William Marwood: The Gentleman Executioner

- DEREK MATHEWS -

The life and executions of William Marwood, the Lincolnshire hangman, who introduced the long drop, the split trap door and a table of length of drops for instantaneous death at executions.

FASTPRINT PUBLISHING
PETERBOROUGH, ENGLAND

www.fast-print.net/store.php

William Marwood : The Gentleman Executioner
Copyright © Derek Matthews 2010

All rights reserved

No part of this book may be reproduced in any
form by photocopying or any electronic or mechanical
means, including information storage or retrieval systems,
without permission in writing from both the copyright
owner and the publisher of the book

ISBN 978-184426-809-2

First published 2010 by
FASTPRINT PUBLISHING
Peterborough, England.

An environmentally friendly book printed and bound in England
by www.printondemand-worldwide.com

This book is made entirely of chain-of-custody materials

To William

Contents

Acknowledgements		ix
Introduction		xi
Foreword		xiii
Chapter 1	The early days	1
Chapter 2	His first executions	24
Chapter 3	His first year as number one	46
Chapter 4	Executions 1875	58
Chapter 5	Executions 1876	78
Chapter 6	Executions 1877	101
Chapter 7	Executions 1878	116
Chapter 8	Executions 1879	130
Chapter 9	Executions 1880	165
Chapter 10	Executions 1881	209
Chapter 11	Executions 1882	223
Chapter 12	Executions 1883	245
Chapter 13	Conclusion	263
Appendix 1		269
Appendix 2		271
Appendix 3		277

Acknowledgements

In order to complete this work I would like to thank the following:

The invaluable help of the staff of the Lincolnshire Archives, the Nottingham central Library Archives, the Bolton Library Archives, Walkden Library Archives, Salford Library Archives, Manchester Library Archives, Dundee Library Archives, Local Studies Department Cardiff Central Library, Records Museum Leicester, Chester Local History Archives, Exeter Local History Library, York Local History Library, Edinburgh Local History Library, Usk Library Archives, Kent Local History Archives, Leeds Local History Archives, Taunton Local History Archives, the Old Bailey Archives, Horncastle Library, Derby Local Studies Library, the British National Library, London, Durham History Library, Northwich Local History Library, Aylesbury Local History Library, the Liverpool Records Office, the Wiltshire Local History Library Archives, Roy Hallam of

Old Bolingbroke, John Knight of Goulceby, John Hibbert.

My special thanks go to the following newspapers and magazines, which have allowed me to use their articles:
The Fife Post,
The Northampton Journal,
The Berrows Journal,
Worcester Journal,
The Gloucester Journal,
The Bolton Journal,
The Derby Evening Gazette,
The Liverpool Echo,
Inverness Journal,
The Farnworth Journal,
The Durham Journal,
The Western Mail,
Leicester Mercury,
The Daily Telegraph,
The Sunderland Echo,
The Nottingham Journal,
Lincoln, Rutland and Stamford Mercury,
The Edinburgh Scotsman,
The Echo,
Clare Record, Ireland,
The Irish Times and The Times, U.K.
Lincolnshire Life.

Extra special thanks go to:
Frances Raftery.
Manchester and Glasgow Police Museums,
Seamus Breathnach, http//www.irish-criminology.com,
My wife Patricia,
The publishers.

Introduction

It was about eighteen years ago when my thoughts turned to writing a book about executioners. I started by researching every executioner I could find anything about, writing on and off between other books.

The title of my book on executioners was to be 'The Suspense is Killing Me.' It went up to almost one hundred and fifty thousand words and then I realised that most of the executioners had had something written about them already so I abandoned the project, although I still have it on file.

Four years ago, while I was doing some home improvements, I got it out and realised that William Marwood, the man who brought the long drop to the country, who invented the split trap door and who drew up a table of what length the rope should be to ensure almost instantaneous death, had never had a book written about him.

During weekend breaks away up and down the country, I started going into library archives and collecting more information on the man in question. I started writing.

This book is the result.

Foreword

Born of poor parents William Marwood became known throughout England and Ireland as 'The Gentleman Executioner.' He was a master shoemaker by trade from Horncastle who in 1869 made up his mind to become an executioner.

He had over the years taken a great interest in the 'art' of hanging and felt that it could be improved. He had never hanged anyone nor even assisted at an execution but at the age of fifty-four he persuaded the authorities at Lincoln prison to let him carry out trials on their gallows. The governor was impressed and asked him to carry out the hanging of William Frederick Horry on April 1st, 1872.

The execution went off without a hitch and the Governor gave him a letter to use if Marwood ever wanted to procure other execution employment.

In 1874 the Sheriffs of London and Middlesex appointed Marwood as the official number one executioner replacing Calcraft. He received a retainer of twenty pounds per annum plus ten pounds for each execution, but unlike Calcraft, got no actual salary. Marwood was also able to keep the condemned person's clothes and received travelling expenses. The rail system was so advanced by this time that he could travel anywhere in the country with ease, making it possible for him to carry out most of the executions within England and Ireland. He worked without an assistant for most executions but one assumes that if needed, the warders were there to assist him.

William Marwood was something of a celebrity. There was a famous rhyme about him which went like this:

"If Pa killed Ma, who'd kill Pa? Marwood."

He even had business cards printed with the words William Marwood, Public Executioner, Horncastle, Lincolnshire and the words 'Crown Office' over the door of his little cobbler's shop. At the Great August Fair in Horncastle, horse dealers from many parts of Britain and the Continent came and paid sixpence to look at Marwood's paraphernalia. He also made a huge profit selling bootlaces. Marwood declared that his customers were pleased to pay an inflated price to be able to claim they had bought them from the public executioner.

Marwood introduced the 'long drop' method of hanging. He realised that if the prisoner was to be given a drop of six to ten feet depending upon his height and weight and with the noose correctly positioned, death would be 'nearly instantaneous' due to the neck being broken. The long drop removed all the gruesome struggling and convulsing from the proceedings and was undoubtedly far less cruel to the prisoner and far less trying to the governors and staff of the prison, who since the abolition of public hangings in 1868 had to witness the spectacle at close quarters. Marwood was also credited with the invention of the split trapdoor.

In eleven years he hanged one hundred and eighty people including eight women.

Three of his most notable cases were: Charles Peace, a burglar and murderer whom he hanged on February 25th, 1879, at Armley Goal in Leeds: Kate Webster, an Irish servant girl who murdered her mistress and cut up her body, whom he hanged on July 29th, 1879, and Percy Lefroy Mapleton who murdered Isaac Fredrick Gold on a train on the Brighton Line so that he could steal his watch and some coins. Marwood hanged him on November 29th, 1881.

Marwood travelled to Ireland disguised as a clergyman in his role as executioner when he had the job of executing Joe Brady and four other members of 'The Invincible' gang for the murders of Lord Frederick Cavendish and his undersecretary, Thomas Henry Burke in Phoenix Park, Dublin.

William Marwood died on September 4th, 1883, after a very short illness of inflammation of the lungs aggravated by jaundice. This was perceived to be the outcome of a chill contracted while on official duties. His age was recorded as being sixty-five.

Chapter 1 – The Early Days

A Lincolnshire Life article of January 1969, p 12, tells us that, "William Marwood junior was born at Goulceby, Lincolnshire, six miles north of Horncastle on 8th, November 1818, of poor parents. His father, who was illiterate was also a shoemaker had a large family of ten children. William was the third son and the second one to be named William after his father, the first son William dying in 1810."

Goulceby (also found as Goulsby) is both a village and parish in the Wolds, seven miles southwest of Louth and six miles north of Horncastle, bounded on the west by the River Bain. Asterby parish is to the east and Ranby parish to the west. The parish covers just under 1,200 acres (and was slightly larger before 1900). When William was born the population of the village was around two hundred persons.

William Junior attended the free Sunday school in the village, where he learned to read and write. (Not quite grammatically as you will see later, as this book contains several of the letters he sent out to procure executions.)

All the letters reproduced in this book are in their original form, as are the items from the newspapers and magazines.

Prior to 1808 there were few schools. Most of those that existed were run by the church, with emphasis on religious education. Thereafter, William lived his life believing that whatever was written in the Bible was literally true. Most schools at this time used the Monitorial System. There was no direct instruction from the teacher. Older children, often in their teens, were monitors who taught the actual lessons and carried out testing. There were no 'grades or levels' - all ages performed the same work.

William grew up to be a strong child and when he was old enough he was apprenticed to a miller. He broke his leg in the course of his employment and the resulting limp meant he could no longer do the work he was required to do. Thus his father decided to train him up to be a shoemaker like himself. William Junior was a quick learner and soon became as accomplished as his father. After he finished his training his father set him up in a shop of his own at the other side of the village. At the age of eighteen, William married Jessie Lilley who was born in 1811 in the town of Horncastle. They were married on February 15th, 1836, in All Saint's Church, Goulceby.

In his twenties William and his wife moved to the village of Old Bolingbroke where he opened a small cobbler's shop. The village of Old Bolingbroke originated in the Anglo Saxon era in the fifth and sixth centuries. The name means 'the brook of the people of Bulla'. The brook referred to flows through the village to the east of the castle. In 1086 Bolingbroke was first recorded in the Domesday Book as a thriving village. The castle in the village was built around 1232. William became a local preacher in the Wesleyan Chapel that still stands in the village today.

In 1855 Mr and Mrs Marwood moved to the village of Horncastle and lived at 149, Foundry Street with his wife's parents. Quite soon after they arrived in the village William opened a small shoemakers shop in Shoemakers Yard, South Street. He and his wife became regulars of the Wesleyan Chapel in the village and their severance from that sect was rather curious. At the services, one of the members said "their uttering during the responses were very loud and misplaced, they rendered themselves a positive nuisance and as they were getting on everybody's nerves they were asked to leave." In the village, William was looked upon as a man of learning and he gave his advice freely to all those who asked for it. Although he had no children of his own William was not neglectful of the children of the village. He was known to organise races for them along the Wong, with the older ones being handicapped by being placed at the back.

In July 1867, his wife, Jessie passed away and she was buried in the grounds of Holy Trinity Churchyard on Spilsby Road.

William married his second wife Elen Andrews at the Wesleyan Chapel in Queen Street in October 1867 and they moved in to 64 Foundry Street. Their house was furnished in a comfortable, unpretentious style; on one side of the fireplace was a bookcase that was well stocked with medical books. The walls were hung with pictures and nearly all were of Biblical history, the largest being a steel engraving of 'The Last Supper,' another 'The Crucifixion' and a third 'I am the Light of the World'.

Elen Marwood was a quietly spoken woman who always made herself conspicuous by going around the village wearing a coalscuttle bonnet. She was very well versed in the history of criminals and had witnessed a double execution in Leeds in 1849. She always read on Sundays after church about the executions that Calcraft had done. She was to say later that her husband had always entertained a desire to familiarise himself with medical science, and that he had been a devoted student of scientific works before she met him. Why William turned his attention to the repulsive duty of the finisher of the law, she did not know. He detested idleness and worked day after day in his little shop and said when he read the Sunday paper about the criminals, "Had they been brought up in the fear of God they would never have gone wrong."

In 1866 Samuel Haughton, an Irish doctor, devised the original equations for hanging as a humane method of execution, whereby the neck was broken at the time of the drop, so that the condemned person did not slowly strangle to death as in the short drop method of execution. His system became known as the 'standard drop.'

The 'short drop' method of hanging, was carried by placing the condemned prisoner on the back of a cart, horse or other vehicle, with the noose around the neck, the object was then moved away, leaving the person dangling from the rope. The person died of strangulation, which typically took between ten and twenty minutes. Before 1850 this was the main method of execution. The 'short drop' was the one that Calcraft used. His ropes were between two and three feet long.

The standard drop length was between four and six feet, which was arrived at using calculations in English units using the body weight with a drop of 1,260 lb force. The standard drop was considered superior to the short drop because it was intended to be enough to break the person's neck, causing immediate paralysis and immobilisation. It came into use from 1866.

At least four years before Calcraft was retired, Marwood started taking a great interest in the 'science' of hanging. Based on Haughton's article which he had read, Marwood felt that it could be improved. He started practising execution on sacks of corn and later, on pigs and sheep. He realised the position of the rope was critical. By placing the rope on the left under the ear the 2nd or 3rd vertebra would be broken and death would be almost instantaneous. Previously the rope was positioned anywhere and the condemned usually died of strangulation. Marwood practised his famous long drop technique in Lindsey Court, which was close to his shop in Horncastle.

He called his system the 'long drop.'

It was also known as the 'measured drop'. Instead of everyone falling the same standard distance, the person's height, weight and strength were used to determine how much slack would be provided in the rope so the distance dropped would be enough to ensure the neck was broken, but not so much that the person was decapitated. In between 1892 and 1913 the length of the drop was shortened and after 1913 other factors were also taken into consideration, and the drop force was reduced to about 1,000 lbf. (See drop table appendix 1)

In 1874 when Marwood was appointed executioner there was no school for executioners as there was in Pierrepoint and Allen's time. There were no engineers who told William to take notes. There was no 'Old Bill' (a dummy), to practise on. There was no training of how to put the noose on correctly. There were no guides or tables to say the approximate length of drop a person should be given, nor Home Office orders to tell Marwood that the length of the drop should exceed more than eight feet six inches. There was no one to tell him how to carry out a double or triple execution, nor a governor standing at the door of the condemned cell with a stopwatch in his hand. No wait of weeks for the letter to arrive telling him if he was a capable person to carry out an execution. In those days most of the time there were no assistants to help Marwood. He just had to get on with it and carry out the job himself. If no hangmen were available, the Sheriffs had to find someone to execute the culprit even if it meant using one of the prisoners who were to be hanged themselves. These were then given a pardon to do the job on a regular basis.

William Marwood got the job as hangman through his own persistence. Up to then he had led a quiet life serving the cobbling needs of the community. He was convinced that the 'long drop' would be a more humane service and wrote to the governor of Lincoln Gaol asking if he could try out his system on a proper gallows. Since the gallows in his gaol were seldom used the governor allowed Marwood to use it. The Governor was most impressed and allowed Marwood to execute the next criminal at his gaol.

A few days before the trial of Frederick Horry the Sheriff of Lincoln wrote to Marwood to tell him to be ready to execute his first criminal. When Marwood received the letter he packed his Gladstone bag with all his trappings and told his wife he was going away on some shop business. He got the train and made his way to Lincoln to observe the criminal in the witness box.

At the end of the trial the judge put on the black cap and gave out the sentence: "William Frederick Horry. The sentence is that you be taken hence to the place where you have been last confined and from thence to a place of execution, and there be hanged by the neck until you shall be dead; and that your body may be afterwards buried within the precincts of the prison in which you shall have been confined after your conviction. And may the Lord have mercy on your soul." Horry was hanged the next day.

After 1947 the words were changed slightly to:

"The sentence of the Court upon you is, that you be taken from this place to a lawful prison and thence to a place of execution and that you be hanged by the neck until you are dead; and that your body be afterwards buried within the precincts of the prison. May the Lord have mercy on your soul, Amen."

Great August Horncastle Fair, where horse dealers from many parts of Britain and the Continent paid sixpence to look at Marwood's official paraphernalia, he also made a profit selling boot laces which he declared his customers were pleased to pay an inflated price for to be able to claim they had bought them from the public executioner.

The gravestone of William, Marwood's older brother,
who died when he was six years of age in 1810.
Today it can be found in the old graveyard in Goulceby.

The old All Saint's Church, Goulceby, where William Marwood attended school and got married.

William Marwood senior's second marriage record dated 8th, July 1835 and William Marwood Junior's first marriage record dated 15th, February 1836 Goulceby, Lincoln.

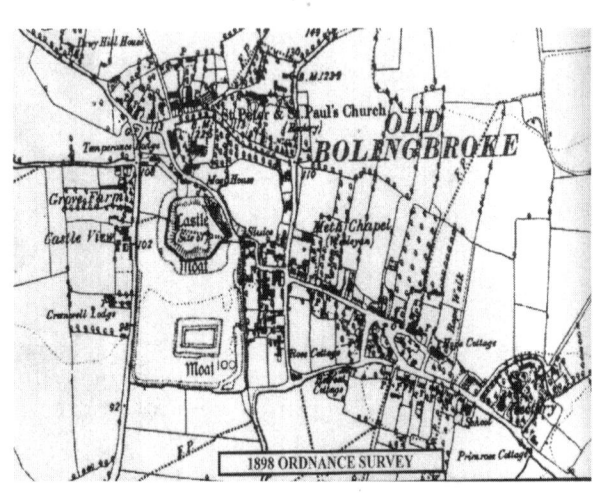

The streets plan of Old Bolingbroke where Marwood and his wife moved to in his twenties.

The Wesleyan Methodist Chapel where Marwood
preached in Old Bolingbroke.
It is still standing in the village today.

The Horncastle roadside plaque, at the entrance to the village where Marwood moved to in 1855.

Corner of South Street, Marwood's first shop in the village of Horncastle.

Marwood's house, 64 Foundry Street, Horncastle.

Plaque outside the door of 64 Foundry Street, Horncastle.

Marwood's little cobbler's shop, on Church Lane, Horncastle.

The blue plaque above the old doorway of Marwood's shop.

Lincoln Gaol and Court House
Where Horry was tried and sent for execution.

William Frederick Horry's gravestone in the Lucy Tower
of Lincoln Castle.
He was Marwood's first execution.

Manchester Strangeways Prison completed in 1869. Marwood carried out eight executions as number one here and his first as assistant with Calcraft on December 30th, 1872.

Execution of Kate Webster July 1879.

Chapter 2 – His First Executions

At the age of fifty-four Marwood efficiently executed his first criminal, William Frederick Horry, a twenty-eight year old publican from Bursley. Horry was born in Boston, Lincolnshire in 1843. When the railways reached the town in 1848 his parents enjoyed using the train to take him to visit friends in the Potteries and to the village of Wolstanton. When he was old enough Horry started using the train himself. In Wolstanton he met and started courting a girl called Jane, a barmaid at the George Hotel. Horry vowed one day that he would marry her and for a wedding present would buy the hotel and they would run it together.

They got married in 1866 and as promised they moved into the hotel. The Horry's were a happy couple having three children within five years. He then started drinking with the customers which turned him into an alcoholic. After many years of rows over his excessive drinking Horry started accusing his wife of infidelity with the customers. Unable to cope with running the public house, the children and her husband's mood swings, Jane moved in with his father in Boston, taking the children with her. Horry stayed at the public house and tried to run it on his own but without success. The public house started loosing money so he sold up and moved to Nottingham.

Because of his bad temper when he went to visit his children, Horry's father banned him from seeing them again. Being banned from seeing his wife and children over the Christmas period Horry got more depressed. He went into town, bought a gun and went to face his wife. Not being allowed in the house Horry shot Jane at point blank range, and waited for the police to appear. He was arrested at the scene of the crime.

At his trial Horry tried to prove that he was insane but the prosecution proved otherwise. He was found guilty and was told he would hang the next day. According to the Governor, the execution went smoothly and Marwood's method greatly impressed all those who were present. After an hour Horry's body was taken down and examined by the surgeons and they, too, were impressed about how the neck was broken. Horry's body was laid to rest within the grounds of Lincoln Castle and a stone was laid giving his initials and the date of his death. This can still be seen today along with many of the other criminals' graves in the Lucy Tower at Lincoln Castle.

From the very start Marwood decided that whenever he was going to execute anybody he would turn his victims to the west, not allowing them to have a

Christian ending by facing the east. Thus he fixed the knot under the left side of the ear.

On August 22nd, 1872, Marwood received a letter from Charles Mahon, Sheriff of Cork, Ireland, asking him if on September 11th, he would execute Thomas Heynes who murdered his wife Ellen. Marwood wrote back agreeing but he never turned up to carry out the execution.

Thomas Heynes was a farmer from Inneshannon, County Cork, convicted of the murder of his wife Ellen. On March 25th, 1872, during a drunken quarrel he stabbed her several times. As she lay bleeding on the ground, he proceeded to kick her to death. Heynes made a vain attempt to cheat the gallows by trying to cut his own throat. When Marwood failed to arrive at the prison, two local men carried out the execution. Their identities were kept secret.

Marwood's next execution was as an assistant to William Calcraft at Manchester Strangeways Prison, December 30th, 1872, using the name of Smith. Marwood knew that his wife read the newspapers about the executions that Calcraft carried out and he did not want her to see his own in print. Marwood had previously informed her he was going away on shop business. The condemned prisoner was Michael Kennedy who had shot his wife at point blank range for refusing to give him a kiss because he had been drinking. Happily married for thirty-five years and having seven children, Michael and Ann Kennedy seemed a happy couple. After one of their children died, things took a turn for the worse when Michael started to get drunk every weekend. This resulted in many rows in the household, even more so when he lost his job. After a drinking bout in his local public house Michael purchased a gun and some ammunition. As his meal was not on the table when he got home, there was a terrible row and he then went to have a sleep on his bed. When he got up he asked his wife for a kiss and she refused his attentions. At this Michael took offence and taking the gun out of his pocket shot Ann in the head. She was taken to hospital where she died three days later from the injuries. Michael Kennedy was charged with her murder.

At his trial his defence claimed that he had taken to drink, lost his job and that the combination of both had made him mad and dangerous. Kennedy pleaded insanity but the prosecution proved that it was premeditated and he was sentenced to death.

The execution was carried out at Manchester Strangeways Prison on December 30th, 1872. Kennedy submitted passively to the hangmen but after the drop fell he was seen to struggle on the end of the rope for several seconds before he died.

In April 1873, Marwood wrote a letter to the County Prison, Dundee asking if the governor would consider using his services for a forthcoming execution.

The Dundee Local Archives supplied this letter:

22 April 1873
South Street
Horncastle Lincolnshire
England

To The Governor, County Prison, Dundee Scotland

"Sir pleas I beg your pardon in riting to you again to now if you are in the wants of a Man as Executioner at Dundee as i understand that thear is a prisoner to be executed on the 29th inst. Sir if my service is wanted on the 29th i have all Things Ready for the execution if thea are wanted. Sir Pleas Will you be so Kind as to Look after this Matter for me the Senance of the Law shall be Caried out in Due Form by me as Executioner.

Pleas Will you be so kind as o send me a Anser Back by the return of post i shall Esteem it a Great Fravour. For the time is geting near for the execution. Sir Pleas i wait your replie Sir i remain your Most Humble Servant, William Marwood"

Since they never sent a reply, we can only presume he never got the job.

Marwood's next execution, recorded as taking place at Derby on August 4th, 1873, was that of Benjamin Hudson aged twenty-four, for the murder of his wife Elizabeth, at West Handley, Derbyshire.

Hudson was a collier, sentenced to death at Derby Assizes on July 15th, 1873, for the murder of Elizabeth. She was found battered to death with a hedge stake at West Handley, near Stavely. Elizabeth had left her husband on Easter Sunday, ten days before the murder. On April 24th, Hudson was seen in the area where she was living and later that night her body was found battered to death in a field. He was soon arrested and charged with murder.

At his trial, Hudson pleaded guilty to causing his wife's death but was instructed by his counsel to change his plea to 'not guilty.' Hudson was found guilty and all attempts at a reprieve proved futile.

The execution was the first private execution to be held at Derby after the 'Execution within Prisons' Act of 1868 and was held inside the gaol, three clear Sundays from the day the sentenced was passed. Under the provision of the Act, attendance was restricted to the Governor of the Prison, the Sheriff's officers, wardens and representatives of the press.

The Derby Evening News supplied the following report:

"Ben Hudson slept soundly on the Sunday night, awakening at five o'clock on Monday morning, when he asked the warders if he could shake hands with five other prisoners with whom he had made an acquaintance. It was raining heavily while the execution took place. Benjamin was dressed in the prison uniform. He carried his prison cap in his left hand and a beautiful bouquet of flowers in his right, which had been given to him by an aunt.

He was conducted to the pinioning room - a grey wooden shed used by the turnkeys. This was only a few yards from the scaffold that was twenty yards to the right of the Gaol entrance. The hangman was already there. Hudson did not seem at all startled to see him. Ben was the second person to be executed by Marwood who was at the beginning of his career, being on the point of taking over from William Calcraft. This was probably to Ben's advantage, as Calcraft had been inefficient and his patients were often throttled to death by the rope rather than dying quickly. William Marwood was more scientific in his approach - he drew up a table of weights and heights which helped him to calculate the length of rope needed to secure an instantaneous death.

Inside the gaol the silence was intense.

The Chaplain and Ben walked first, followed by the High Sheriff, his deputy and six wardens. Ben walked to the scaffold with his eyes firmly on the ground.

The scaffold consisted of a wooden platform about twelve feet square, in the middle of which was a drop two and a half feet deep. Above this was an iron framework that supported the crossbar. Calmly, Benjamin climbed the steps to the scaffold and mounted a pair of steps placed upon 'the drop' level with the suspended noose. This extra height brought his neck level with the suspended noose. Despite his insecure position, he waited calmly while the executioner pinioned his feet, drew a white hood over his head and face and adjusted the noose around his neck.

For about half a minute the only sound to be heard was the unsteady voice of the chaplain, reading the service and the rain pattering on the umbrellas of the witnesses. The hangman stood by a lever, about two yards from the drop. As the prison clock struck eight o'clock, the lever was pulled and the drop fell with a crash.

The writhing body dangled in mid air. After a few moments, the bouquet fell from his grasp, but though spasms went through the body for ten minutes, causing violent movements of the hands and arms, his left hand retained the cap. The black flag was raised at the exact time of the execution and remained there for the prescribed one hour. After Hudson had been pronounced dead, his body was taken down and placed in a crude coffin and taken to the inquest room, and then he was buried in a corner of the prison yard retained for murderers and covered with quick lime.

Special trains were laid on and people walked miles to be present when an execution took place, even when the hangings were no longer public. A good deal of drunkenness was common after the event. On this occasion several hundred people had gathered outside to hear the bell toll, to see the black flag hoisted and to be read the notice of the execution pinned to the door of the prison. Some people had loitered around the gates since the previous evening. The crowd was decorous and sympathetic and nearly all commiserated with the unfortunate Hudson. The waiting crowd heard the distinct sound of the drop as its awful crash delivered Benjamin Hudson to eternity."

Marwood's next execution is recorded as taking place on the August 26th, 1873, at Omagh, Ireland. To get there he had to leave home three days before the execution was due and because of the long trip to Ireland, again he made an excuse to his wife that he was going away on shop business.

Thomas Hartley Montgomery a Sub-Inspector in the Royal Irish Constabulary, once worked in the Northern Bank of Ireland in Newtown Stewart, where he had become friends with a bank teller called William Glass whom he subsequently murdered with a bill hook and then stole some of the banks funds.

On the August 27th, 1872, William Glass was totalling up the takings in the bank at Omagh when Thomas Hartly Montgomery entered. He stayed there till closing time and then left. At 4.15pm a member of the public saw the door of the bank was open and went inside. He rang the alarm after he found the teller's body lying behind the door, covered in blood.

Several policemen from the Royal Irish Constabulary, including Sub-Inspector Thomas Hartley Montgomery, arrived and inquiries were made. It was reported that Montgomery was the last person to be seen coming from the bank after it had closed.

Glass's body was taken to the local doctor where a post mortem was carried out.

A count of the money was made the following morning and £1600 was found to be missing.

Because Thomas Hartley Montgomery was the last person known to leave the premises, he was arrested and appeared at three trials. At the third trial in August 1873, it emerged that at the time of the murder and robbery, he was deeply in debt. The money was found buried in a wood close by.

The first witness to be called at he trial said he saw the accused Montgomery coming from the bank carrying a package. The second witness was a local farmer who had seen Montgomery walking quickly towards the woods where the money was found. The third witness was also an inspector in the Royal Irish Constabulary who told the court he had seen Montgomery in the woods in the vicinity of where the money was found.

The jury took just a few minutes to find Sub-Inspector Thomas Hartley Montgomery guilty. He pleaded insanity but the judge refused his plea and sentenced him to be hanged on the August 26th. Montgomery was asked if he had anything to say and he admitted he was guilty of the murder. He said, "the first blow I struck with a billhook, caught Glass's head and as he tried to escape by the door I struck him twelve more times to finish him off."

On the morning of the execution several members of the press were admitted to the gaol to write their reports.

The report from The Irish Times states:

"At a few moments to nine Montgomery walked towards the scaffold accompanied by the reverend and the governor and his officials, then Marwood the hangman.

Montgomery was dressed in tweed trousers and a dark blue coat, he looked ghastly pale and he loudly said the Lords Prayer. On reaching the scaffold he faltered but was led on by the executioner, once on the scaffold he was strapped around the ankles and the hood and rope were put in position and the trap was released. Death was instant with the exception of a kick from his left leg."

On the day of the hanging another hangman, George Smith was present in just case he was needed. Later in the day Marwood made his way to the ferry for the long journey back to Horncastle.

After a while Marwood moved his cobbler's business from South Street, to number 6, Church Street, which adjoined the churchyard and in the neighbourhood of 'Hangman's Corner.' The records state that the gallows at 'Hangman's Corner' was there in 1230 and was last used in 1232. Marwood took on an assistant at his shop and when he was trained up to his satisfaction he put him in another shop on Boston Road. By his skilled labour, the cheapness of his products and the fluency of his speech, William Marwood speedily attracted a considerable number of clients to his shop. He became renowned not only for good workmanship but as a man who could tell a funny tale and make an hour pass pleasantly.

On September 8th, 1873, Marwood assisted Calcraft again with the execution of James Connor at Kirkdale Prison, Liverpool. On this occasion the rope broke and Marwood and the priest had to go down into the pit to get Connor out and re-hang him with a new rope.

Connor was a powerfully built London boilerman who was sentenced to death by Mr Justice Brett on August 16th, for the murder of Sheffield-born James Gaffrey and the attempted murder of William Metcalfe on Monday, August 11th. Connor had been drinking and visited a music hall in Liverpool. On leaving the theatre, he made conversation with Mrs Mary Shears, the wife of a ship's steward and asked her to join him for a drink. When she refused he began to get violent and accused her of stealing money from him.

Gaffrey and Metcalfe were walking down Mill Street, Liverpool, when they saw Connor strike the woman. They rushed over and asked him what was going on. During the ensuing row Connor struck Gaffrey in the face. When Gaffrey responded by punching him back, Connor drew a knife and stabbed him behind the ear, then turned on Metcalfe, wounding him.

Connor pleaded manslaughter through provocation but was convicted of murder.

It was another in the long line of botched executions by Calcraft, the aged hangman.

From the Liverpool Echo, dated September 8th, 1873:

"This morning James Connor, who was condemned to death at the last Liverpool Assizes, was executed within the precincts of Kirkdale Gaol, under circumstances which painfully affected those whose duty it was to witness and take part in it. The scene was one which had no parallel in the criminal annals of Liverpool. Up till the hour appointed for the execution there was no indication of anything unusual. On the contrary, it was reported that the convict had slept well during the night and awoke with composure at half past five in the morning. About half an hour afterwards his spiritual adviser, Father Bonte who administered the sacrament according to the rites of the Roman Catholic Church visited him. Connor then partook of a hearty breakfast, and appeared by his demeanour to have prepared himself to undergo with firmness the last preparations of the law. He engaged in his devotions with great solemnity, but without exhibiting the least sign of nervousness. When informed of the approach of the fatal hour he submitted to be pinioned with perfect calmness, and there was no traces of excitement save in the ghastly pallor of his face, and a determined pressure of his bloodless lips. He then walked from his cell to the scaffold in the company of Calcraft, the executioner and other prison officials. His step was steady and elastic, and his manner so self-possessed that he seemed to be the least moved of any of the persons present.

The spectators comprised only the Under-Sheriff, the Governor of the gaol, the Chaplain, the Roman Catholic priest, the representatives of the press and a few of the warders of the prison. When he was at length placed upon the mark, his courage remained unshaken, and at the moment when Calcraft was adjusting the noose the convict nodded smilingly to two of the warders who were standing at an angle of the prison yard. The cap was then pulled over his face, the executioner shook the hand of the culprit, and the bolt was withdrawn. To the astonishment, however, of the bystanders, the unhappy man disappeared through the trap, and a dangling piece of rope was seen swaying in the air. Frightful yells arose from below, and it was discovered that the cord had snapped. The culprit was found doubled up in a hole beneath the fatal drop, utterly unable to move hand or foot in consequence of the straps which bound him. Several of the warders rushed to his assistance, and after Marwood and the priest extracted him from his position, placed him in a chair. The poor creature was in a dreadful state of consternation and probably in pain, for though he must have fallen on his feet, the distance was sufficiently great to give a severe shock to the system. The priest came forward and endeavoured to soothe his agitation as he sat for a period of eight minutes waiting until a new rope had been procured. The alteration in his manner as he sat on the gibbet during this painful delay was very marked. He seemed to be seized with a new desire for life; his fortitude completely gave way; and he gazed about with piteous wildness, as if imploring mercy. A notion appeared to have presented itself to his bewildered fancy that the penalty of his crime had been already duly paid. The priest besought him to be calm, and to keep up, to which the wretched man replied – "I stood it like a brick the first time, and I shall get off now; surely this is enough." Among other mutterings he was heard to say, "What do you call this? Do you call this murder? I stood it bravely, didn't I? You will let me off, won't you? Let me off do." But hanging by the neck till dead meant what it said, and a new rope was quickly found and it was fixed round his neck then he dropped a second time. This time the rope didn't snap and justice had been done."

As Calcraft was declining in years, and it became known the Government was in want of a new hangman, Marwood was invited to Newgate to demonstrate his long drop, and did so to the authorities' satisfaction.

In 1874 Marwood became the new executioner of the Sheriffs of London and Middlesex and introduced a number of innovations to the ancient craft: he improved the pinions, began using a pliable, thinner five-ply Italian silk hemp rope instead of Calcraft's stiff and thicker shorter rope. He also invented a brass eye for his noose, and finally developed a table of weights and drops from which any executioner could calculate the correct long drop for a person, based on the individual's height and weight.

Marwood served as hangman for nine years, showing concern for and good manners toward his victims at all times. He became something of a celebrity, carrying out executions all over England and Ireland. The Times reported that every time he crossed the St. George's Channel two detectives would always accompany him. He was the first executioner not to be paid a salary, but a fee for each appointment. By putting Marwood on a retainer of twenty pounds per annum and a ten pounds fee for every execution the Sheriffs of London and Middlesex were on to a good thing when we look at the perks of the hangman of Inverness in 1833.

The following report was taken from the Inverness Journal newspaper dated 1907:

"The Last Inverness Executioner. It is now nearly 75 years since the Inverness Town Council dispensed with the services of a salaried executioner. His removal was one of the first fruits of the 'Burgh Reform Act. In December 1833, the Council resolved that the appointment must cease. The post of hangman was Mr Donald Ross, of Inverness, who made it a remunerative one. He was appointed executioner in 1812, with a salary of £16 per annum. There were, says the 'Dundee

Courier' fees and perquisites independent of salary, and Donald had various bites and nibbles at the public purse.

First, he was provided with a house, bed and bedding; second, he was allowed 36 peat's weekly from the tackerman per the petty customs; third, he had a bushel of coals out of every cargo of English coal imported into the town; fourth he was allowed a piece of coal as large as he could carry out of every cargo of Scottish coal; fifth he had a peck of oatmeal out of every hundred tons landed at the shore; sixth he had a fish out of every creel or basket of fish brought to the market; seventh he had a penny for every sack of oatmeal sold at the market; eighth he had a peck of salt out of every cargo; ninth he was allowed every year a suit of clothes, two shirts, two pairs of stockings, a hat, and two pairs of shoes. Added to these fixed and regular sources of income.

Donald levied blackmail on the lieges in the shape of Christmas boxes. And had besides a sum of £5 at every execution at which he presided. These items must have amounted to £50 or £60 per annum, and as there had been just three executions since Donald was appointed they must have cost the town nearly £400 pounds per execution."

In the pictures section of this book one can see the gallows which were used in Glasgow until 1868 when the passing of the Act giving the authorities power to hold executions in private was carried out. The accuracy of the picture is guaranteed by the fact that it has been drawn from a sketch by the gentleman who in 1869 broke up this gruesome structure for firewood. As you will see, there was ample provision made for brisk business, and three persons could have been executed at the same time. Whether a triple execution took place on it is unknown, but double executions were fairly common.

In 1853 Hans McFarlane and Helen Blackwood were executed together for the murder of a man. In 1828 and 1830 double executions also took place, the victims having been sentenced for assault and robbery.

As will be seen from the illustration, the gallows was moved on wheels. When not in use it was kept out of sight in a building in East Clyde Street where the police station now stands. When an execution was to take place this great lumbering vehicle of ominous purpose was dragged from its concealment and placed right in front of the steps leading up to the Justice Building in Jail Square. This was done during the night, and everything was in readiness for the execution, which took place at eight o'clock in the morning. The stair of the gallows was placed on the steps leading to the Justice Buildings, so that the execution party had only to leave the Court precincts to mount the fatal platform. To the right of the picture you can see the lever which, the hangman pulled to set free the trapdoor, precipitating the unhappy wretches to their doom.

The length of the rope was fixed at seven feet whatever the weight of the persons so that their bodies hung down in the chamber below, their dying agonies being mercifully concealed from public gaze. Then, after a sufficient time had elapsed to ensure that the requirements of the law had been carried out, the hangman opened the door under the stair of the gallows, and brought out the bodies. It is known that Tam Young, the last hangman in the service of the city of Glasgow, used this gallows when he had any work to perform.

Its last condemned was the notorious Dr Pritchard, whose execution on July 28th, 1865, it was said to have been witnessed by over a hundred thousand people. The executioner on that occasion was William Calcraft but instead of using a long rope, took out one of his short ones and used that instead.

It was reported in the Edinburgh Scotsman:

"He did not die without a struggle. For an instant after the drawing of the bolt no motion was perceptible, but soon it swung quickly round, the whole form quivering and the hands working with muscular action. Another reporter described Pritchard's final contortions as 'after the bolt was drawn he shrugged his shoulders for more than half a dozen times, his head shook and his whole body trembled violently.'

The body remained hanging until fourteen minutes to nine, when Calcraft proceeded to lower it. In doing so he lost his grip and the body fell suddenly and violently on to the coffin which was resting on two trestles below. Part of the coffin bottom was knocked out by the fall but fortunately it was repaired by a number of workmen who were present at the execution."

Marwood was the first executioner to conduct almost all of his executions within the confines of prison walls. He was also the last executioner to work when each prison was allowed to construct its own gallows of different designs. He was an exhibitionist on the scaffold and he played the press for all they were worth – an 1881 account from the Daily Telegraph gives a good example:

"As we filed into the yard, I noticed that we were being one by one saluted by a somewhat diminutive man clothed in brown cloth and bearing in his arms a quantity of leather straps. There was nothing apparently in common between the grave and the gallows and the man, and for the moment I imagined that the individual who raised his hat and greeted each arrival with a 'good morning, gentlemen', was a groom who had chanced to pass through the place, bearing a horse's bridle and gear, and who was anxious to be civil. But to my horror, the man in the brown coat proved to be no stranger wandering about in the manner I had pictured, but the designer of the horrible structure on the right, and the official most closely connected with that and the open grave, William Marwood it was who thus bade us welcome, and the straps on his arms were nothing less than his 'tackle'.

I confess to a shudder as I looked upon the girdle and arm pieces that had duty on so many a struggling wretch, and half expected that the man who carried them would have attempted to hide them. But no such thing! To him they were implements of high merit, and together with the gallows formed what he now confidentially informed his hearers was 'an excellent arrangement'. It was evident that in the gallows and the tackle too he had more than a little pride. He was even ready to explain with much volubility the awful instruments of his craft.

"That rope that you see there", quoth he, as he gazed admiringly at the crossbar of black wood, "is two and a half inches round. I've hung nine with it, and it's the same I used yesterday." Nor does he manifest the quaver of a muscle as he went on to point to certain peculiarities of the design in his machinery of death. Had he been exhibiting a cooking apparatus, a patent incubator, or a corn mill, he could not have been more complacent or calmer. "It's the running noose, you see," said he, "with a thimble that fits under the chin."

"The pits all new," he went on to say; "new brickwork, you will see, and made for the purpose." A glance revealed it was all new – new as the grave. Formed after the ideas of Marwood himself, it certainly appeared to be as an engine of death. It consisted of two pits, connected with each other, one broad and the other a narrow oblong, the broad one being immediately under the gallows, and covered by a black trapdoor that opened in the centre and was only supported by a long bolt; the other contained a brick staircase that led under the gallows.

Above the trapdoor, or rather at the right hand side of it, and close by the gallows tree, was a lever, something like a switch handle that one sees on railway lines, connected with the vault below the trapdoor. The rope that hung from the crossbar was coiled up; and although it had done duty so frequently, as Marwood had said, seemed nearly new.

To Marwood the whole thing evidently seemed a triumph of art; and as he moves hither and thither, explaining the superiorities of his design, he evidently expected that his handiwork would meet approval. All the while the bell dismally tolled. At length a warder came battling up, and with a bundle of keys in his hand beckoned to Marwood. It wanted about 10 minutes to 9 o'clock, and the doomed man was waiting.

"Ready for you," remarked the warder, and with an expectant look Marwood gathered up his 'tackle' and followed. With an easy skip and a hop, as though we were answering an agreeable call, he left us and disappeared towards the cell of the man about to die."

Marwood enjoyed his fame, having a sign above his little shop with the words; 'Marwood Crown Office' and exhibited several of his used ropes inside. He also had cards printed by rubber stamp announcing 'William Marwood, Executioner, Church Lane, Lincolnshire, England.' He gave these to everyone he met. He also made a good living selling bootlaces at three pence a pair to all who came to see him at his shop. This shop and his house can still be seen today in the town of Horncastle, Lincolnshire.

Horncastle, when associated with the name of Marwood in newspaper reports of executions, is invariably designated as a small village. This, however, is scarcely correct.

From the Farnworth Journal 1879, a reporter writes:

"Although its population is somewhat under 5,000, the place has good claims to the title of a town. In the shape of public buildings, besides numerous excellent business establishments, there is a Corn Exchange, a County Court, a Mechanical Institute, a Dispensary, a Free Grammar school, a Sessions House and a large Gas Works. Horncastle has also a commodious Workhouse, it being the capital of a 'Soke and Union' comprising of fifty-eight parishes. The principle part of the town is built within an angle formed by the confluence of the small rivers Bain and Waring. Hangman's Corner is on the Eastern boundary of the parish, at which public executions were formally carried out is in the vicinity of his shop."

The town is approached by a single track railway from Kirkstead and is the terminus. The traffic from the villages beyond was very considerable. The last passenger rail service from Horncastle ran in 1954, with complete closure to freight traffic in 1971. Horncastle's railway station was demolished in the 1980s and the site is now a housing estate.

Chapter Three – His First Year As Number One

In his first year as Number One executioner Marwood carried out thirteen executions and travelled the length and breadth of the country. His first three executions of the year were on January 5th, 1874, at Durham, where he executed Charles Dawson, William Thompson and Edward Gough.

Charles Dawson's crime was committed on September 13th, 1873. Dawson and his mistress, Mrs Martha Jane Addison lived as man and wife at Darlington. On September 13th, 1872, they went out to the local public house with the three people who shared their house. As the night went on Dawson started an argument with Martha that the collar on his shirt was too tight so he punched her. She left him in the public house with his friends, whilst she went off to another public house with her friends.

On his way home Dawson saw Martha in the street with her friends and took his revenge by hitting her with the bottle of beer he was taking back to the house. She fell to the ground and he began to stamp on her. Her friends tried to stop him, but to no avail, and she died at the scene of the crime. The police were called and he was arrested and charged with murder. At his trial he pleaded to manslaughter, but the jury found him guilty as charged and the judge sentenced him to be executed.

Edward Gough was the second condemned man. His crime occurred on July 7th, 1873.

James Partridge, a pitman, was drinking with a group of friends in a public house at Sunnyside, County Durham when in walked Edward Gough, another pitman from the same pit, who ordered a small porter. Joking with him, Partridge told Gough not to order a small drink but a large one and to share it with him. Gough drank up and left the public house. After a while Gough came back with a friend, challenged Partridge to a fight and they went outside. Just as Partridge was taking off his jacket, Gough pulled a knife from his pocket and stabbed Partridge in the groin. Before help could arrive Partridge died and Gough was arrested and charged with his murder. At his trial he pleaded to manslaughter under provocation but the jury rejected his plea. The judge placed on the black cap and sentenced him to death.

The third criminal to be executed on that day was William Thompson for the murder of Mrs Jane Thompson, his wife.

This article is from the Durham Journal:

"Twenty-six year old William Thompson was a pitman convicted of the murder of Mrs Jane Thompson who was only twenty, with whom he lived at Anfield Plain. They had travelled into Newcastle during the afternoon of October 4th, 1873 and began to argue after he saw her talking to another man. They returned home and got ready to go out that night. When her father, who lived with them, went on ahead to the pub, he again started an argument over the man he had seen her talking to earlier. They made up and went out drinking, but later whilst drunk he accused her of being unfaithful and cut her throat.

A neighbour hearing the commotion went to see what the noise was about and saw her lying dead on the floor. The police were called and William was charge with murder. At his trial he showed no remorse for what he had done and went to the gallows with a smile upon his face."

Marwood's fourth execution of the year took place at Newgate on June 29th, 1874. The person he was to execute was a female Mrs Frances Stewart. Her Christian name recorded at the trial was the male version Francis. She was Marwood's first woman victim and the first woman to be hanged in the new execution shed at Newgate and also the first woman to be hanged by the long drop method. Was she Marwood's first blunder? The Echo report of the execution quotes; "He did not tighten the noose sufficiently and she struggled somewhat at the end of the drop."

This article is from the Times:

"Frances Stewart or Fanny, as she liked to be known, was a forty three year old widow; she lived with her daughter and son-in-law at 4 Lordship Place, Chelsea, London. Her son-in-law accused her of breaking the door of a hen house and there was a quarrel during which he told her to leave his house for good. On the evening of April 28th, she was nowhere to be seen. Neither was her daughter's baby. Frances had taken it and stayed the night with a friend. She left there the following morning and wandered the streets of London all day with the baby. They were both very tired and were taken in by another friend who told her to take the baby home to its mother.

On May 1st, Frances pushed a note through her younger daughter's door and later went to see her where she declared "I have done a murder, I want you to give me into the hands of the police." She was arrested and taken before a magistrate and held at Newgate where her daughter visited her. She told the daughter that she had been crossing Albert Bridge and put the baby on the parapet to rest her arms and lost her grip on the child who fell into the river below. A waterman near Millwall dock found a baby's body in the river and it was confirmed that it was her daughter's.

Frances's trial took place on June 10th. She was convicted of murder but the jury added a recommendation for mercy, which was disallowed."

Marwood's fifth execution of the year was carried out at Exeter on August 10th. The person he had to execute was John MacDonald.

On June 28th, John Macdonald started a quarrel with Mrs Walsh with whom he lived whilst her husband was at sea. The quarrel was over some furniture they had bought together. She said it belonged to her and it caused a fight, ending up with her on the ground and Macdonald on top of her with one hand round her throat and in the other brandishing a poker. Mrs Walsh's son came home and, on hearing the commotion, ran to her aid dragging Macdonald off his mother. Macdonald went to spend the night with a friend.

The next morning he went to the shops and bought some poison, burst into Mrs Walsh's house and battered her to death with a bedpost. A neighbour heard the commotion and called for the police. Before they arrived Macdonald drank the poison and tried to cut his own throat. He was arrested at the scene, and was taken to the local prison, treated and made a full recovery. At his trial he pleaded that he was insanely jealous because his lover had been unfaithful to him. After Macdonald was convicted of murder and awaiting his execution, he made two further attempts at taking his own life without success. Marwood however, made sure that he died on the gallows.

The Exeter prison was described in Vincent's Guide to Exeter, 1884 thus:

"The prison is built on the Pentonville, or 'silent' system. Every prisoner has a separate cell, about 13 feet by 7 feet, and contains water, washing bowl, bed, table, stool, etc. and a gas jet. The cells are well ventilated and the vitiated air is carried off by an extracting flue. The foods for the inmates are delivered through flaps. There is a bell-pull, which strikes upon a gong and throws back a plate with the number of the cell, when the prisoner requires the attendance of a warder, in the case of sickness or otherwise.

The exercise yards are arranged into radiating compartments to prevent the prisoners communicating with each other. The officer in charge has an inspection house in the centre, so as to have the whole of the prisoners under his eye whilst taking exercise. The chapel has also radiating seats so contrived that the prisoners are precluded from seeing each other. The superior advantages attending the separate system of prison discipline, has caused it to be generally adopted in new prisons."

Marwood's sixth execution of the year took place at Usk, near Pontypool on August 24th, 1874. The person he had to execute was James Henry Gibbs for the murder of his wife, Sarah Ann.

On June 3rd, a farmer discovered a partly decomposed body in a ditch on a farm at Llanrumney Hall, near Cardiff. It had been partly eaten by insects and he called the police. Investigations led the police to her husband, a butler at the hall, who was later charged with her murder. The state of the body made it difficult for doctors to be certain of the cause of death but Gibbs probably killed her by cutting her throat as there was evidence of neck injuries on the rotting corpse. Mr Justice Lush at the Monmouth Assizes sentenced James Henry Gibbs to death. Gibbs protested his innocence and maintained it in the death cell until the hangman called for him to leave. Gibbs then broke down and began to wail pitifully as he was assisted to the scaffold by two warders where he had to be held erect until the drop fell.

A newspaper correspondent described Marwood and the journey to Usk:

"This is Mr. Calcraft's successor, he is a man of middle height, of pale face, a narrow forehead, dabs of baldness here and there upon his head, a fringe of dark whisker, a clean shaven chin, restless eyes which never look straight at you, thin lips, a dull, vulpine smile. When I last saw him his coat looked as though it had been laid on a block and chopped into shape with an axe. His hat was alarmingly cylindrical as to the body, and ludicrously narrow as to the brim.

A suggestion of a shirt collar struggled to make itself apparent through the intricate doublings of a huge black neck wrapper. A snake-net of chains meandered over the waistcoat; a gem ring glittered on the forefinger. A gentleman who had "required his services had given the latter to him" and therefore he had prized it much. He would receive £10 for hanging the man tomorrow, and about 50s. for his travelling expenses. When he had concluded the present engagement he said he would go to Liverpool to hang two other men.

At a roadside station a young mother, with a child, got into the carriage. Mr Marwood became very effusive. He took the child upon his knee. He kissed it and he allowed it to play with his watch and to finger his ring. He produced peppermint lozenges from his pocket, and put the same into the infant's mouth. At the same time he clutched a lean carpetbag that, from experience, I knew to contain (1) a rope; (2) another rope; (3) a comb;

(4) a shirt. Under his arm he throttled an old and wheezy umbrella – and altogether you would have taken him for a liberationist lecturer. He was a most benevolent and bland gentleman. He talked about the weather and the crops. He prophesied that we "should have a hard winter;" and lamented that workingmen should remain in unobtrusive poverty.

To all these very respectable and old-gentlemanly propositions did the young mother seriously incline? She did not accept them merely – she swallowed them. At last we reached Usk, and almost before I had time to realise the fact my "elevating" friend had slipped from the carriage and was walking along the road at a terrific pace with a man who could only have been a policeman in plain clothes.

Usk lay sleeping lazily in the sunlight as the hangman, with his shambling walk, crept along the white road towards the solid square building, which seemed like a huge blot on one of the loveliest landscapes in England. It was Sunday, and evening. Little knots of people loitered on the bridge close to the prison, watched as he passed by, then he rang the bell at the portal of the prison, his arrival was a welcome one, for no other man would undertake the ghastly work he had to fulfil.

On walking past the prison you could hear the hammering as the scaffold was being constructed; and from a little window almost hidden away in a corner you could see the pale face of a boy murderer peeping out. From the little church upon the hill there came the merry chime of bells. The inner portion of the gaol was made gay with flowerbeds, and the whole place looked like an old chateau in Brittany, carefully tended and much prized.

As the bell on the church on the hill chimed a dull tone, the man died an agonising death which even to the onlookers seemed an eternity, when it was all over Mr Marwood took his ticket to the station, his umbrella throttled under his arm, and his carpetbag as before, and boarded the train and again took the occasion to remark that things were very brisk in the execution business."

Marwood only had two days at his home in Horncastle before he was off again, this time to Liverpool for the execution of two prisoners, the female, Mary Williams, who murdered Nicholas Manning and the male Henry Flanagan for the alleged murder of his aunt whilst attempting to rape her. Flanagan was heard boasting to a friend that he had stolen some money - three sovereigns – from her. Flanagan was arrested and during his two day trial made the excuse that he was drunk at the time and could not remember anything of what had happened to her. He was found guilty and sentenced to be hanged.

Mary Williams's crime was the murder of Nicholas Manning by shooting, in an act of revenge over something he had done to her.

Henry Flanagan was executed first whilst Mary was held in her cell. Once Flanagan's body was taken down the trap was reset and she was brought to the gallows and hanged on the same rope. Both died instantly and they were buried in the grounds of the jail.

Marwood's ninth execution of the year was at Horsemonger's Lane (Later known as Surrey County Gaol) on October 13th, 1874. The person he had to execute was John Walker Coppon, a coffee house owner who murdered his wife. For some unknown reason John Coppon came home drunk from the coffee house and his wife put him to bed, then spent the night in another bedroom. When John got up the next morning he went to his next-door neighbour's house and borrowed a butcher's knife and returned to his house. Whilst his wife was getting ready to leave for her work, Coppon rushed at her with the knife and stabbed her to death. The neighbour heard screams, went to investigate and found her body in the bedroom. Coppon was sitting on the bed, the knife still in his hand.

The police were sent for and he was arrested and brought to the court at the Old Bailey where he claimed she had aggravated him. "I was angry because my wife would not perform her wifely duties and sleep in my bed with me. She even told me she would do the same again." Coppon swore that the crime had not been premeditated but since the knife had been obtained just prior to the attack, this suggested to the jury that it was and they returned a verdict of guilty as charged. October 13th, 1874, was not a lucky day for him as he swung from the rope.

After a month of running his shoe shop, attending to his garden and enjoying himself, Marwood was off again, this time to Winchester where he had to execute Thomas Smith for the murder of Captain Bird at Aldershot Barracks. Smith was a private in the 20th Hussars. On September 13th, 1874, Smith stated to the police that

Captain Bird had given him excessive punishment. He was seen going to his billet and picking up his gun then he shot the officer dead. At his trial his defence tried to prove there was no malice between them but they were unsuccessful and he was hanged on November 16th, 1874.

Marwood had Christmas Day at home and on December 26th, he left for Durham where he had an appointment to execute Hugh Daley on December 28th, for the murder of Philip Burdey. One night in a small mining village near Durham, Hugh Daley who had been drinking after work, swayed through the streets on his way home. When he got there his wife and a next-door neighbour put him to bed. Another neighbour named Philip Burdley called in to see how he was. Their talking woke up Daley and he got out of bed. On the way to see who was talking to his wife he picked up a poker and chased Burdley into the street. Getting him into a corner, Daley beat Burdley for over two hours. He died at the scene. Daley was arrested for his murder and executed on December 28th, 1874, in the southeast corner of Durham Gaol in the presence of a dozen witnesses.

The newspaper reported he walked firmly to the scaffold without any assistance where, on the drop, confessed his crime to the executioner. Outside the prison fifty persons stood and watched until the black flag was hoisted above the gaol. They then dispersed.

From there Marwood caught the first train he could to Staffordshire where he had to execute Robert Taylor on December 29th, 1874. Robert's crime was the murder of Mary Kidd for giving him two pence instead of the half crown he asked for. On November 23rd, Mary Kidd and a girl, Sarah Hollis, were approaching Coppice woods when they spotted Taylor sitting on a fence. He asked Mary for some money and she said she only had a few pence. He asked her for half a crown, but she gave him the two pence telling him that it was all she had. Taylor pulled out a knife and stabbed her in the neck. As he was going towards Sarah, a cart came along and frightened him off. Mary died at the scene. A description was given to the police and later Taylor was picked up and identified by Sarah. The trial took place at the Staffordshire Assizes and with a guilty charge he was sentenced to hang on December 29th. It was reported in the local newspapers that his last words were "Snap me off quickly." When the drop fell he died instantly. After the execution Marwood left the jail and headed for home to spend New Year's Eve and New Year's Day with his wife.

Chapter Four – Executions 1875

For Marwood, 1875 was an extremely busy year for he had twenty-one executions to carry out before the year came to an end. Although he had managed to spend New Years Eve and Day with his wife, in the early morning of January 3rd, he was off on his travels again, this time to Newgate to execute James Cranwell.

James Cranwell was a shoemaker like Marwood. Cranwell invited his girl friend, Emma Bellamy, round to his house in Great James Street on Saturday October 17th, 1874, for tea then attacked her.

At his trial in December 1874 it was revealed that firstly he hit her with a hammer then he cut her throat with a large knife. The neighbours testified that they heard noises coming from Cranwell's bedroom and went to investigate. After knocking at his door for some minutes, Cranwell opened it and he was covered in blood. At the bottom of the stairs they saw his girlfriend.

She had come out of the bedroom, staggered down the stairs and collapsed. Another neighbour called the police and Cranwell was arrested. Emma was taken to the hospital where she died some time later that evening. Cranwell pleaded insanity but it was dismissed and he was sentenced to hang on January 4th, 1875.

After a couple of months at home looking after his shoemaking business Marwood had to go to Sligo, Ireland to execute John McDaid who was convicted for the murder of Edward Ferguson, a retired butter merchant, on October 31st, 1874. Edward Ferguson's niece had not seen him for a few days and went round to his house to check on him, but the house was locked up. She asked the police to gain entry to the property and his body was found. He had been beaten to death and various valuable items were missing from the house. McDaid had sold these items just a few days earlier. He was arrested, sent for trial, found guilty and executed on March 24th, 1875.

Four days later Marwood was in Chelmsford for the execution of Richard Coates. Coates was sentenced to death on March 8th, for the murder of Alice Boughen. After attempting to violate her in a school closet he beat her to death to stop her talking about the matter. Then he tried to throw her body into a nearby river but because he could not lift it over some railings decided to take it back to the school. On the way back Coates, was seen by a passing policeman who arrested and charged him with Alice's murder. Coates confessed to Marwood in the condemned cell saying "he did it because of drink." Just before nine o'clock on the morning of March 29th, Coates was led out to the gallows and hanged.

The next day March 30th, 1875, Marwood was in Maidstone for the execution of John Morgan who murdered John Foulson in a hut by slitting his throat. Morgan was a nineteen-year old bandsman in the 82nd Regiment who was convicted at Maidstone Assizes on March 6th, of the murder of John Foulson. The two soldiers were in the same regiment, stationed at Shornecliffe camp. On the night of the crime they were sitting in a hut with two young drummers. Morgan gave one of the drummers a sum of money to go and buy some sweets and both the drummers left. Within seconds of them leaving the hut, Foulson rushed out clutching his neck and dashed into another hut where he picked up a pen and wrote "Morgan done it". He died within minutes from the hideous gash. His last action was to point accusingly at his killer who had now entered the hut.

Morgan denied the crime, claiming that Foulson had committed suicide, but this was easily disproved by cuts to the victim's hands, caused while trying to fend off the blows. Morgan wrote a last letter from his cell asking his former comrades to forgive him for the shame he had brought on the regiment. Marwood executed him on March 30th.

Marwood's next execution took place at Clonmel, County South Tipperary, Ireland on April 9th, 1875. It was that of John Russell who murdered William Sandford.

On Saturday, April 10th, 1875, Marwood wrote a letter to his wife Elen from Birmingham.

"Dear Elen

This is to say that i sent a letter on Thousday Last on my arrival at Clonmal in ireland to say that i was all well – now this i to say That i left Dublin last night about 9 a Clock for Hollehead arrived about 3 a clock this morning for Birmingham arrived about 11 a clock to day i ham now in Birmingham with the governor wating to see the governor of Bristol at half Past Tow to day and then i leave hear for Cambridge this after noon all Well so if all well i shall Retorn on Monday night or Tusday Morning i hope all is well at Home Tell my Poor Boy Nero that is Marster is Coming home rember me to Mi Moodey i hope she will call on Sunday and take Tea now take good cair of my Poor nero be good to Polley i hope i shall find all Things Right on my retorn my Trust is god he is my great helper all thing are in is ands he as maid my was throw the wartery Deeps and Throw Mountains high Valleys Raised so i shall Praise the Lord most high si i Conclude at Presant Thine Truley Wm Marwood."

Marwood's sixth execution of 1875 was carried out at Liverpool on April 19th, when he executed Alfred Thomas Heap who was an unqualified chemist. He was convicted at Manchester Assizes of the murder of Margaret McKivert who died after he tried to procure an abortion for her.

After Margaret McKivert became pregnant her mother suggested she should go to see the druggist Alfred Heap who had a shop in West Gorton, Manchester, to ask him if he could do anything for her. On March 13th, 1875, Margaret and her mother went to the shop to see him. Mrs Carroll, his housekeeper saw Heap take both of them upstairs and she heard noises of a struggle. After a while she saw Margaret and her mother come down and leave the shop. In the afternoon Heap was seen making up some packages and putting them in his pocket. Later that day Heap and Margaret met at a public house where he was seen passing the packages over to her. She paid him a pound note.

After arriving home Margaret took the contents of the packages and went up to bed. Next morning she was violently sick and over the next few days got worse. Margaret's mother went round to the shop and asked Heap to come and take a look at her.

He arrived later in the day just as Margaret's mother was attending to her. Margaret gradually got worse and she passed away on March 18th. Margaret's doctor was summoned and he declared she had been poisoned. Heap was arrested along with his housekeeper, who was later released with no charges put against her. At Heap's trial Mrs McKivert (the mother) stated that as he was standing by her daughter's bed he was jeering at Margaret saying, "she mustn't die on him". Evidence was brought to the trial that in 1867 he served five years in jail for a similar incident, although on that occasion his victim had lived.

The Manchester Guardian, August 1867, states:

"Alfred Thomas Heap, was indicted for having, at Gorton, on May 1st, attempting, by means of an instrument, to procure the miscarriage of Sarah Ann Lunn. The case occupied the Court several hours, but the evidence was wholly unfit for publication. The prisoner was found guilty. The sentence of the Court was that he be kept in penal servitude for a period of five years.

The trial for the murder of Margaret McKivert took place at the Liverpool Assizes on Friday April 2nd, 1875, the jury convicted Heap of Margaret's murder, but they added a strong recommendation for mercy. The judge put on the black cap and sentenced him to death at Kirkdale House of Correction, Liverpool. The date for the execution was fixed for April 19th. Many letters were sent to the Home Secretary asking for a reprieve but he reported that there were no sufficient grounds to justify this."

A report from Liverpool Echo states:

"On the day before the execution Marwood arrived at the gaol. At a few minutes before eight o'clock on the morning of the execution the prison bell began to toll and members of the press were allowed into the gaol yard to witness the execution. At eight o'clock Heap walked up the steps of the scaffold and calmly looked up at the rope hanging from the beam. He listened to the Reverend while the leg straps were put on. The bolt was drawn and Heap was dead. The drop given by Marwood was around five feet. After the black flag was raised, the large crowd, which had assemble outside the jail, quietly dispersed."

Marwood had a few days at home with his wife and dog, Nero, before he had to leave again for Bristol to execute William Hale for murdering his wife.

Both William Hale and his wife suffered from drink problems and they were always quarrelling. One night when Hale returned home drunk from the public house he found his wife standing on the doorstep. She was also drunk but refused to go into the house with him. Hale opened the door and went into the kitchen, pulled a knife from the drawer and went back to the doorstep plunging it into her neck twice. She died on the spot. At his trial, Hale pleaded provocation but the jury did not believe him and brought in a charge of guilty. He was sentenced to death and hanged on April 26th, 1875.

On July 27th, 1875, Marwood was in Warwickshire for the execution of Jeremiah Corkery who allegedly stabbed PC Lines and PC Fletcher.

On the 7th March, PC Lines and PC Fletcher called into a Birmingham public house and arrested a man for burglary. As they took the man away, a group of his friends, led by Corkery, began taunting the officers as they headed from the pub. One of the men was seen by a witness to draw a knife during the disturbance and both officers were subsequently stabbed. Although the witness couldn't positively identify the man, he claimed that the attacker had been struck over the head with PC Lines' truncheon. Corkery received treatment for a head wound later that night. The next morning, a group of men including Corkery were paraded before the wounded officers at the hospital, but Corkery wasn't picked out as the assailant and was released. On March 20th, 1875, PC

Lines died and soon afterwards Corkery was arrested and charged with PC Lines murder. Corkery protested his innocence but was convicted despite PC Lines being unable to identify the attacker plus a lack of any other evidence linking him with the crime. Corkery convicted at Warwick Assizes by Mr Justice Field, and declined the court's offer of mercy as he maintained his innocence but the execution went ahead as planned. The four other men who were with Corkery at the time received life sentences.

On the August 2nd, 1875, Marwood was in Durham to carry out three executions. It would have been four but another murderer was spared as he was classed as insane and was sent to Broadmoor prison.

Marwood's first execution was Michael Gillingham for the murder, without provocation, of John Kiegoam, a young Irishman. John Kiegoam was set upon by a gang of six youths at Darlington on April 10th. Witnesses testified they saw Gillingham strike the man about the head with a sharp instrument, which punctured his brain over the eyebrow. At his trial Gillingham swore that he was innocent of the charges against him but the jury just took fifteen minutes to pronounce a verdict of guilty as charged. The judge then put on the black cap and in passing sentence said, "I am satisfied from the evidence that the jury has arrived at a proper verdict. You committed a fellow man into the other world without the least chance of preparation but more consideration will be offered to you than you gave him. You will have an advantage in the prison of spiritual advice, and I implore you to throw aside any hope that mercy will be extended to you, and prepare for the expiation of your crime by your death on the scaffold." Gillingham was led away, never again tasting freedom. He was executed three weeks later.

Marwood's second execution was that of William McHugh, who was sentenced to death on July 13th, for the murder of Thomas Mooney at Barnard Castle by throwing him into the River Tees. His accomplice, a Mr William Gallagher, refused to assist him and he was acquitted.

This report was written in the Durham Journal after the executions:

"William McHugh was sentenced to death at Durham Assizes on July 13th, 1875, for the murder of Thomas Mooney at Barnard Castle. Early on the morning of April 11th, a witness saw McHugh and another man, William Gallagher, dragging Mooney down to a yard, where he was then thrown over a wall into the River Tees. As the victim was either drunk, or insensible due to a blow to the head, he was unable to swim and drowned in the murky water. Gallagher had refused at the last minute to help McHugh throw the man into the river, and as a result he was acquitted, although the judge censured him for not stopping McHugh committing murder.

Marwood's third execution was that of Mrs Elizabeth Pearson for murdering her uncle, James W. Watson with rat poison put in his medicine. Elizabeth Pearson was convicted at the Summer Assizes of 1875, of the wilful murder of her uncle, James Watson at Gainford, Durham. She was acting as a housekeeper for her uncle, after the death of his wife. Soon she started stealing from him and decided to get rid of him, presumably in the hope of an inheritance from him. To this end, she added a strychnine- based rat poison to his medicine which had the desired effect. The death had all the classic signs of strychnine poisoning and his son, Robert, was suspicious and obtained a post-mortem. Elizabeth began to empty the house of its contents, further casting suspicion on herself. James Watson's stomach contents revealed large quantities of strychnine and iron cyanide.

At her trial, Elizabeth's lawyer contended that she had no motive for killing her uncle and that the poison must have been given to James by their lodger, who had since left the area. The jury were unimpressed with this and brought in a guilty verdict within an hour.

At just after eight o'clock in the morning William Marwood launched Gillingham, McHugh and Elizabeth Pearson into eternity. Elizabeth was buried on August 2nd, 1875, in an unmarked grave next to Mary Ann Cotton. Mary Ann Cotton was Britain's first female serial killer who poisoned her victims with arsenic. Thomas Askem and William Calcraft hanged her on Monday, March 24th, 1873.

On August 9th, 1875, Marwood was in Lincoln for the execution of Peter Blanchard who murdered Louisa Hodgson with a knife. Blanchard, a Lincolnshire tanner, had been trying in vain to court Louisa Hodgson, a girl of twenty-two. She wouldn't go out with him, partly because he wasn't liked by her parents and also because she had recently begun seeing another man in the town. On March 7th, 1875, Louisa and her new boyfriend were walking home from church when they came across

Blanchard. He walked down the street with them until he reached his front door, where he pulled out a knife and stabbed Louisa through her heart. He was immediately detained and admitted he had committed the crime due to jealousy. On August 9th, 1875, he was executed within the prison walls of Lincoln Castle at nine o'clock. He expressed no wish or desire that the sentence of the law should not be carried out right up to the time of his execution.

The report which follows appeared in the Lincoln Mercury:

"On the Saturday prior to the execution taking place, his father and mother and other relatives visited him, the parting was very touching. Shortly before the hour of the execution a thunderstorm broke over the city, and the procession proceeded to the scaffold as the storm raged, all present were drenched. The culprit walked with a firm step and ascended the scaffold with a firm step without assistance. After the execution the black flag was hoisted on the watchtower. After the body was taken down it was buried alongside the other murderers in the keep."

When William Marwood had an execution to carry out in Lincoln he always stayed with Mr West, landlord of the Portland Arms. For many years after Marwood's death there were ropes belonging to him hanging in the bar.

At the execution of Peter Blanchard on August 9th, 1875, Marwood was recognised by a neighbour who let the whole town of Horncastle know he was the hangman and there was quite a furore in the town. On one occasion a neighbour said to a reporter, "after it was known, people would follow him everywhere howling so much that he had to appeal to the station master for protection. Another time on an omnibus the passengers would not rub shoulders with him, and threatened to overturn the vehicle if he did not leave it. He was viewed with such loathsomeness by the higher classes that a number of gentlemen set afoot a movement to drive him from the town, but of course they could not rob him of his rights as a citizen. After a while the feelings died away and he was allowed to go about his business without molestation. He did however avoid the public's gaze and left earlier than necessary when going to executions. This was the first time Elen knew that her husband was an executioner and after that day she refused to even let him have his Gladstone bag in the house and said he had to keep all his trappings in the shop."

Marwood's next execution was at St. Helier, Jersey on August 11th. The person he had to execute was Joseph Philip Le Brun who murdered his sister.

Marwood described his journey. "I took the first train from the little station in Horncastle to make my way down to Weymouth where I arrived in the early evening. After a hearty meal I made my way to the quayside and boarded the steam packet which sailed at 2am. After breakfast on board the steam packet, I went to the prison where Joseph Le Brun was being held and got a good look at my victim. I did my calculations and got the rope ready. And then went to look at the gallows which was on Gallows Hill. It was to be a public execution the very first one I had done, all others before that were carried out in private. The next day the prisoner was led through the streets with the halter around his neck up to Gallows hill where the execution took place in front of a large crowd."

The local newspapers carried the story of the man Le Brun who was to be executed:

"A murder without a motive is meaningless, as well as intriguing. If there is no motive, the police must be sure they have arrested the right man. So did Joseph Le Brun really kill his sister and wound his brother-in-law at their home in St. Helier, Jersey, on the evening of December 15th 1874?

The facts were very simple. Le Brun, who was usually drunk, was absolutely sober that day. As was his habit, he had dinner with his sister Nancy and her husband Philip Laurens that evening, and because his brother-in-law had to go out, he stayed on longer than usual. At about 8.45pm however, the police were told by an excited neighbour that Nancy Laurens, had been murdered and her husband had been shot. They asked Laurens, who had facial injuries and an arm wound, who had attacked him, and he replied: 'My brother-in-law Joseph shot me.' They found the body of Nancy covered in blood sitting on a sofa. There was a shawl covering her face and her stocking feet were in a bucket of water.

They arrested Le Brun, who was in bed, and took him to the house where Laurens was awaiting a doctor. Laurens called Le Brun a 'hangdog' and asked, 'Why did you fire at me?' Le Brun replied, 'It wasn't me.'

At the inquest on Nancy, Philip Laurens said that when he opened his front door on returning home Le

Brun pointed a gun at him and shot him in the face. I said to him, 'what have you done? You have shot me!' He made no answer. Laurens said he didn't notice his wife on the sofa, but ran to a neighbour, Clement Rondel, for help. The gun, he said, 'was his own, and his brother-in-law often borrowed it.' He had never had the slightest quarrel with Le Brun. He added that 'he had recently received £28 from him (a considerable sum all those years ago), which he had given to his wife for safekeeping, and Le Brun was aware of this.

Le Brun was tried at St. Helier on July 7th, 1875. The suggestion was that he might have killed his sister for £28 fell flat when the court was told that Nancy was drunk nearly every day and he would not have needed to kill her in order to steal the money. The evidence against Le Brun was purely circumstantial; no motive was suggested, there was no blood on his clothes, no powder on his hands and only small change in his pockets. The Attorney General said that although he was unhappy in seeking the death sentence, the penalty if Le Brun was guilty could not be otherwise."

The jury of twenty-four persons unanimously convicted Le Brun of attempting to murder his brother-in-law and then, curiously, said that they couldn't agree about Nancy's murder. Under Jersey law, if five of the jury did not say that Le Brun was innocent he would be declared guilty. The judge asked each juror for his opinion and finally announced that Le Brun had been found guilty by a majority verdict.

Public opinion on the island was horrified. The jury foreman wrote to the Home Secretary seeking a reprieve, as did the lawyer acting for Le Brun's relatives, who pointed out that Philip Laurens and his wife, were 'great drunkards,' and could well have mistaken another man for Le Brun.

There was, however, no reprieve. Joseph Le Brun went calmly to the scaffold on Thursday, August 12th, 1875. The law abolishing public executions in Britain did not extend to the Channel Isles until 1907. Le Brun made history by becoming the last man to be publicly hanged in the Channel Isles and the very first public execution for Marwood.

On August 16th, Marwood was at the other end of the country in the town of Lancaster executing two prisoners. The first execution was of William McCullough who murdered William Watson, a lodger who shared his house with him and his wife. On the evening of March 29th, McCullough came home drunk and asked his wife for more money so that he could go to the public house once more. She refused his request and he started to beat her. Breaking away from him she ran to William Watson's room for protection. As he was calming her down, McCullough went to the kitchen, took a knife and stabbed Watson to death. He was arrested and sentenced to hang.

The second execution was that of Mark Fiddler, an unemployed spinner who cut his wife's throat after she left him to move into lodgings on her own. He sold the house and spent all the money on drink, then went to ask his wife for forgiveness. She refused to listen to him and he cut her throat then he cut his own but he recovered. He was sentenced to hang. The drop opened up the wound and blood poured into the bottom of the pit. Had the drop been a little longer he would have been decapitated.

Marwood's next two executions were at Liverpool's House of Correction on September 6th, 1875. It was another double execution. The first to be executed was William Baker for the murder of Charles Langan. Baker, landlord of The Railway Vaults public house, was drinking in another public house with some friends. When it closed they went on their way to find a club in the area of the docklands to continue drinking. On finding one open they were refused entry because of their condition. Coming out of the club at the time was Charles Langan with his group of friends; Charles and William had had a row a few days earlier. The Baker group followed the Langan group and at a well-lit place Baker pulled out a gun and shot Langan dead. At his trial he pleaded guilty to manslaughter due to drink, but the prosecution proved otherwise.

The second person to be executed was Edward Cooper, a twenty four year old sailor who shot dead the acting second mate, Edward Jones, on board the ship 'Coalbeck.' On April 24th, 1875, Jones gave Cooper an order which he refused to carry out. Cooper went to his cabin and took a gun out of his rucksack and went back to the bridge and shot Jones at point blank range. He was locked in the hold and when the ship got back to Liverpool he was tried and sentenced to hang some eight months after the crime had been committed.

After a month at home, Marwood had to travel to Glasgow for his next execution. The person he had to execute was Patrick Docherty twenty-one year-of-age, who murdered John Miller with a garden hoe during a fight at Rotherglen Bridge, Glasgow.

The Encyclopaedia of Scottish Executions by Seamus Breathnach states:

"When four men and two women began dancing on Rotherglen Bridge, Glasgow, on May Day 1875, it ended in a dance of death. They had all been drinking heavily and as the excitement grew another man, John Miller, a 21-year-old miner, climbed on to a wall to watch them.

Something Miller said apparently annoyed one of the male dancers. Patrick Docherty, and Miller began to snarl at each other. Docherty picked up a hoe and smashed it over Miller's head. Miller was taken to a local hospital where he died from the injury.

Docherty was tried at Glasgow Circuit New Court, where the prosecution claimed it was a deliberate act of murder and the defence argued that it was a blow struck merely on impulse. He was convicted and, despite a recommendation for mercy, was hanged on Tuesday, October 5th, 1875, at Glasgow's Duke Street Prison – the first execution to be held there."

On the same day that Docherty appeared for his trial another man was there named Middleby, also a murderer. For some unknown reason he was reprieved. It was believed that there was a mix up in the system and Docherty was hanged in error.

On October 9th, Marwood was in Dunbarton for the execution of David Wardlaw, a fifty-six year old shoemaker from the town of Bonhill, who murdered his wife with his shoemaker's hammer.

The Encyclopaedia of Scottish Executions by Seamus Breathnach states:

"A 56-year-old shoemaker from Bonhill, Dunbartonshire, Wardlaw ended thirty years of troubled marriage by murdering his wife whilst inebriated. He had no recollection of the crime he did.

At his trial the jury gave him a guilty verdict with a recommendation for mercy. Three attempts were made to the Home office for a reprieve but they were all rejected.

Wardlaw was so poor that the public purse paid for the black suit he wore on the day of the execution. He was executed on the scaffold that had only been built two weeks earlier to hang another criminal Patrick Docherty already mentioned. It was a fifty-yard walk from the condemned cell. For half of this length he kept his eyes on the ground. On the scaffold with his legs pinioned and the cap pulled down the lever was pulled and with a loud grating sound the drop fell and he went to his doom."

The Encyclopaedia of Scottish Executions also states:

"Hangman William Marwood caused a sensation in Dunbarton when after hanging David Wardlaw inside the prison on Tuesday, October 19th, 1875, he submitted his expenses to the local council. He claimed for a dozen bottles of beer, two bottles of whisky and brandy, a bottle of sherry, and a bottle of port, most of which, he said, he drank on the morning of the execution."

On December 21st, Marwood was at Newgate for the execution of Henry Wainwright for the murder and dismemberment of Miss Harriet Louisa Lane at his shop on Whitechaple Road, London. Wainwright was a brush manufacturer and although already married, set up Harriet as his lover in her own home. She began calling herself Mrs King after they had two children. Living above his means he moved her to a cheaper property that she did not like. Leaving the children with a neighbour she went to his shop, and that was the last time she was seen alive. The police started making enquiries and Wainwright stated she had gone to live in Brighton with another man and this, said the police, "was followed by a letter, saying that she had moved abroad."

After being declared bankrupt Wainwright had to move out of his shop and got an employee to help him move some packages. The employee checked some of the packages and found that they contained body parts and he called the police. Wainwright was arrested and brought to trial. At the hearing it was revealed that he had murdered Harriet and he and his brother had cut the body up. Found guilty, Wainwright was sentenced to hang whilst his brother was sentenced to seven years in prison. Wainwright was executed outside Newgate Prison, 'a public execution,' on December 21st, 1875, for the horrendous crime he committed.

The next day December 22nd, Marwood was in Newcastle for the execution of John William Anderson who murdered his wife by stabbing her seven times after an argument because she had decided to leave him due to his drinking.

In August, Anderson, a young clerk, gave up work and took to drink and as a result, the relationship with his wife became strained. They argued constantly and she threatened to leave him unless he got a job. On August 27th, they visited a neighbour and appeared on good terms, but later, when they returned home, another neighbour heard screams from their house. When the disturbance was investigated, Mrs Anderson was found lying in a pool of blood: she had been stabbed seven times. Anderson gave himself up immediately and freely confessed to the murder. He was tried, convicted and was sentenced to be hanged. The sentence was carried out on December 22nd, 1875.

Marwood's last execution of 1875 was carried out at Morpeth, Northumberland on December 23rd. The person he had to execute was Richard Charlton who murdered his wife with a gun after she left him to live with her sister because of his excessive drinking. Charlton was a farm labourer sentenced to death by Mr Justice Denman at Durham Assizes for the murder of his wife. After the birth of their first child in the spring of 1875 Sarah Charlton left her husband because she became tired of him coming home drunk, and went to live with her sister at nearby Dinnington. On June 5th, Charlton went to his sister-in-law's house armed with his gun. After failing to persuade his wife to return home, he shot her dead and seriously injured his sister-in-law before turning the gun on himself. He was incapacitated for a time, due to his self-inflicted wounds. A report in the local paper wrote, "He walked firmly to the scaffold and died instantly at the end of the long drop."

Chapter Five – Executions 1876

Marwood's first execution of 1876 was at Morpeth, Northumberland. The person he had to execute was George Hunter who murdered his friend William Woods with a shotgun after a bout of drinking.

The trial report states that on December 9th, 1875, Hunter and Woods were shooting birds in a local forest and it started snowing so they decided to go and have a drink in a local hostelry. On the way home Woods started throwing snowballs at Hunter who took offence and ordered him to stop or he would shoot him. Woods threw another snowball and Hunter turned, pointed the gun at him and pulled the trigger. Woods died instantly. Hunter pleaded that he thought the gun was empty but it had one round still in the breach. Since Hunter had threatened Woods previously the jury found him guilty of premeditated murder and the judge sentenced him to death. He was executed on March 28th, 1876.

A local newspaper carried this report:

"Hunter was read prayers at half past seven and just before eight o'clock was taken to the prison room where Marwood pinioned him. He showed no sign of fear and required no assistance as the procession moved to the scaffold. The rector read the service and he was placed under the drop – it fell just as the clock struck eight. After an hour he was taken down and an inquest was held. He was buried within the confines of the gaol."

Marwood wrote a letter to the Maidstone Gaol when he arrived home:

"Pleas this is to inform you I shall arive at the Prison on Monday the 3rd day of April all well and bring all the things wanted for the Execution. Sir, Pleas will you be so kind as to make some improvement in the Pitt in the Length of the drop. Pleas will you take out three feet Squair in the Senter of the Pitt and 3 feet Deep of this don it will make a great improvement in the Execution you may depend on me to arive on Monday April the 3rd Day."

Marwood's next execution was on April 4th, at Maidstone. The accused was Thomas Fordred who murdered his illicit lover, Mary Ann Bridge. Fordred was a very jealous man and was often heard saying that he would kill Ann if she ever spoke to another man. On his way home from work he saw her doing just that, he took her to a public house to have a drink and on the way home in a fit of rage kicked her to death.

At his trial he pleaded that she fell over and hit her head on a stone. The prosecution's doctor proved otherwise and Fordred was found guilty and sentenced to be executed. Marwood carried this out on April 4th.

On April 10th, Marwood was in St. Alban's for the execution of George Hill who murdered his illegitimate son, William Thrussel, with a hammer.

When George Hill was served with a maintenance order for his son he had other ideas. He first went to a public house and got drunk, then he went to see the mother and talked her into going to see a house he was prepared to rent for them. On the way to the property he attacked the mother and child with a hammer. The child died whilst the mother survived. Hill was arrested at the scene. When she was well enough to give evidence he went to trial for the murder. After sentence was passed he broke down and pleaded remorse at what he had done. He went to the gallows a broken man. The scaffold had to be specially built for the occasion, at a cost of £36. 9s. 6d. Hill was the last man hanged in the prison, which closed two years later.

On April 24th, Marwood was in the town of Bristol for the execution of Edward Deacon who murdered his wife with an axe. Edward Deacon was another shoemaker. He had been married for nine years but due to his drinking his wife had left him on several occasions. Just before Christmas 1875, they had got back together again and after a couple of weeks she threatened to leave him again if he did not cut down on his drinking. On February 22nd, 1876, he went to a neighbour's house and borrowed an axe to cut some logs. Whilst doing so, the neighbour heard Deacon's wife cursing her husband. In a rage Deacon struck her over the head with the axe, she died at the scene.

At his trial he pleaded he hit her in self-defence, but on the testimony of the stepdaughter, who convinced the jury that this was not the case, he was found guilty and was returned to the jail from where he was to await his fate.

From Bristol Marwood went straight to Cardiff for the execution on April 25th, of Joseph Webber who murdered Edward Stelfox with a double-barrelled gun.

The report that follows comes from the 'Western Mail' March 14th, 1876, supplied by the Local Studies Department, Cardiff Central Library and is reproduced with permission from the newspaper:

"Murder at Cardiff. Early on Monday morning 13 March, the calm of Cardiff life was interrupted by a report, which rapidly spread over the town, to the effect that a most deliberate murder had been committed. Gossips, ever on the alert to catch, enlarge, and extend all exciting topics, made the most of this crime. "There has been a murder", says one; "a deliberate murder!" says the next, and so on, until an affair bad enough in itself, was painted all manner of colours, and classed among the most diabolical of crimes. During this morning the story was told and retold in public houses, in the streetcars and along the street, were various, and all but the truth. It was not until the special issue of the 'Western Mail' was distributed about noon that anything definite was known about the affair, except to the police, who were as reticent as they could be under the circumstances. However, at an early hour it became known that a fisherman named John

Webber had shot another fisherman, named Edward Stelfox, who died from his wounds a few minutes afterwards. It appears that Stelfox, who occupied a well-known shanty on the seashore, at the East Dock and was the proprietor of the public house, No 155, Bute Road, rented fishing privileges from the Bute trustees. During the last year or so the fisherman, John Webber, had encroached upon Stelfox's district, and, as he paid no rent for the privilege, the latter felt indignant, and laid complaints against the conduct of Webber. Webber was at one time in the employ of Stelfox, but he started in business for himself, and has been constantly engaged in poaching on the fishing grounds of which Stelfox was the lessee.

Webber announced his determination to build a shanty close to that of Stelfox, but Stelfox appealed to the dock master, and that threatened menace was avoided. But Webber anchored his fishing smack within the sight of Stelfox's dwelling and announced his determination that it would stay there for the next six months. To this Stelfox objected, and applied to the dock authorities to prohibit encroachment upon his rights. Incensed at this action, Webber, who had already possessed himself of a double-barrelled gun, rose up early and proceeded to the abode of his antagonistic competitor. After addressing a few words to Stelfox, who was in the fish hut, he took deliberate aim and fired the gun at him. The entire contents of the first barrel penetrated his breast and passed right through his lung. As soon as he was shot Stelfox staggered out of the fish hut into the house, which was across a narrow passage about six feet wide.

There he fell into the arms of his house keeper explaining, 'My God, Annie, I am a dead man!'

With determination to make sure of his work, Webber rushed after his victim, pushing against the door, which was instantly bolted by the woman. Finding he could not force it open he stepped two paces to the left, and, smashed the glass in the window with the muzzle of the gun, and fired again, the shot went through Stelfox's thigh near the groin. Stelfox died within a few minutes. Having accomplished his purpose, Webber leisurely walked away to his smack. Some said that he gave himself up, and others said that he was apprehended, they were wrong on both counts. He was, however, arrested a few minutes after seven o'clock by Police Constable Seddon on his smack, and conveyed to the central police station, by the way of the docks and Bute Street. He was eagerly scanned by thousands of people who left their homes and work to catch a glimpse of the man by whose hand Stelfox had fallen.

Shortly after twelve o'clock the prisoner was brought before the magistrates and charged with a capital offence. Council did not represent him. The hearing did not occupy much time, and at length the case was brought to a standstill by the announcement that a post mortem examination had not been made on the body of Stelfox. The prisoner was remanded until later in the week. At the second trial he was found guilty and sentenced to be executed.

At eight o'clock on the morning of April 25th, 1876, John Webber, aged sixty-three was executed within the walls of Cardiff prison. The sentence was carried into effect with the strictest privacy, the representatives of the Press being excluded. Ample precautions were taken that the execution should be witnessed by no persons, other than those authorised to be present, it having come to the knowledge of the gaol authorities that certain portions of the Taff Vale and Rhymney railways overlooked the yard in which the scaffold stood, the managers of the two companies were communicated with and the consequence was an order that during the time of the execution and an hour afterwards no trains should pass over those parts of the line to which the attention had been called. Policemen were stationed on the sloping banks, and to make assurance doubly sure, a timber parapet was raised some distance above the court yard.

The prisoner, who, until a late hour on Monday night was engaged with the chaplain in prayer and religious conversations, slept well, and early on the morning of the execution, rose, dressed himself in his own clothes, and was again occupied for some time in devotional exercises. After he had taken breakfast, the governor entered his cell, accompanied by Marwood, the executioner, and the prisoner was pinioned. He submitted himself to the operation calmly. Then the procession was formed, and Webber was led to the scaffold, which had been constructed in one of the yards near the Taff Vale Railway Station. The prisoner did not require the assistance of the warders, one of which walked on each side. His step was firm, and as the chaplain read the opening part of the burial service, the prisoner repeated portions as he moved along.

When the small procession reached the scaffold, those, which formed it, fell back, and Webber and the executioner stood alone on the 'drop'. The rope was quickly and skilfully fastened round the culprit's neck, and the white cap was drawn over his face, the lever of the 'drop' was touched, and the murderer of Stelfox was a dead man. Almost simultaneously with the drawing of the bolt a black flag of pennon shape was run up on the flag staff above the prison, and the large crowd outside, numbering, it was estimated two to three thousand persons, was made aware that the sentence of the law had been carried into effect.

The bell of the prison and that of St John's Church had been tolling for a quarter of an hour previously, and continued to be tolled for a quarter of an hour after stopped, and the crowd drifted away.

According to the custom the body was allowed to hang for an hour and then removed to a building used as a dissecting room, facing the governors office. In a few minutes after the removal of the body from the drop the scaffold was taken down, and traces of the execution were, as far as possible, swept away. There is, happily, every reason to believe that Webber died penitent, and full of hope of forgiveness hereafter.

Later in the day the body was buried within the walls of the prison where the sentence had been executed.

Marwood, the executioner, left Cardiff almost immediately after he had performed his duty. In an interview he stated, 'the rope with which I hung Webber was the same rope that terminated the career of the notorious Wainwright. It was also used at Newcastle, Maidstone, and twice at Morpeth. A week ago it was employed at the execution at St. Albans, and on Monday

Deacon, the Bristol murderer was hanged with it. It will be used again in Belfast for the execution of another murderer.

With questionable taste some persons living in Cardiff were anxious to obtain it, and before he departed the city they offered him a considerable sum for it, but he refused to part with it. The fee received by the executioner for performing his office upon Webber was £10, in addition to travelling and other expenses."

From Cardiff Marwood travelled to Holyhead to catch the late afternoon ferry to Belfast for the execution on April 26th, of John Daly who murdered Margaret Whiteley by kicking her to death on September 15th, 1875.

Margaret Whiteley was a relative whom Daly took for a drink. After getting quite drunk they returned to his house where he took advantage of her. She threatened to report him to the police and he hit her in the face. She fell to the ground where he kicked her to death and then ran away. When he was caught he was tried at the Belfast Assizes and sentenced to death.

Marwood's next four executions took place at Newgate on May 23rd, where his assistant was hangman Incher.

The crime was mutiny and murder on board the ship 'The Lennie'. The persons they were to execute were George Kadi, aged 22 otherwise known as 'Lips,' Pascaler Caladis, aged 33, otherwise known as 'Big Harry,' Malleo Corgalis aged 36 better known as 'French Peter,' and Giovanni Caccaris, known as 'Joe the Cook.'

'The Lennie' set off from the English shores in 1875 with a crew from all over the world and during the voyage problems began when the captain yelled at the crew after they tangled the ropes during a tack. One of the crew pulled out a knife and killed him. Other members of the crew attacked other officers and killed them also. Van Hoydonck, a steward, tried to save the officers but he was overpowered and locked below the decks. Because they could not navigate the ship, they brought Van Hoydonck back on deck and ordered him to sail to Greece. However, he pointed the ship towards England instead. Just off the coast of France he and a cabin boy put notes in bottles and dropped them overboard. The French navy found them. The mutineers were captured and returned to England to await their fate, which came on May 23rd, 1876.

A report from The Times May 24th, 1876, states:

"Yesterday morning the four men convicted at the last Sessions of the Central Criminal Court, before Mr. Justice Brett were executed within the prison at Newgate. After their trial and conviction the doomed men were said to acknowledge their guilt and the justice of their sentence, adding they must have been tempted by the devil: The sentence was carried out just after eight o'clock in the morning at the back of the prison. Just before eight o'clock the men were introduced to Marwood, the executioner and submitted themselves to the process of pinioning. They had previously written letters to their friends, which they entrusted to the Greek Consul to be forwarded to their relative destinations.

At length – all the necessary arrangements having been completed – the convicts were seen emerging one by one from the gaol to the place of their execution, the prison bell tolling all the while.

First came 'French Peter', next 'Big Harry', then 'Lips' and lastly 'Joe the Cook' each wearing a white calico cap.

'Big Harry' on being placed on the scaffold, said, 'Good Bye, Good bye.' Joe the Cook appeared to realize the doom that awaited him far more acutely than any of the rest, and as the noose was being adjusted seemed to be on the point of fainting. At last, all things were ready, and at a touch by the executioner of the lever, the drop fell with a dreadful crash, and the men, all of whom still in their prime, had expiated their crime with their lives. According to the custom of late years, immediately after the sentence of the law had been carried out, a black flag was hoisted over the roof of the prison, and the bodies of the convicts, after hanging for an hour, were taken down and subsequently submitted to the coroners inquest.

Later that day the dead bodies were placed in a shell of quick lime and were buried within the precincts of the prison."

Marwood's next execution took place at Glasgow on May 31st. The person he had to execute was Thomas Barr who had murdered his mother-in-law with a knife. Barr married Margaret Sloane in 1874, for one reason only – to look after his four children. The marriage only lasted two years before Margaret, then pregnant, moved out to live with her mother, Mrs. Margaret Sloane at her home in Gallowgate, central Glasgow. Barr heard that she was spending time with the two male lodgers and he went to the house to investigate but was refused entry. He went back to the house later in the day, taking a knife with him. He forced the door and stabbed his mother-in-law, Mrs. Sloane, to death and beat his wife so brutally that she died in hospital after giving birth to a stillborn child. Barr then fled the town. He was seen by a policeman in Aberdeen, arrested and brought back to Glasgow to be tried. At his trial he pleaded insanity but the jury rejected his story and he was sentenced to hang in the city's Duke Street Prison on May 31st, 1876.

After having some time at home, Marwood's next execution took place on July 26th, at Durham. The person he had to execute was John Williams who murdered his brother-in-law, John Wales at Edmondsley, near Durham.

On August 1st, 1876, Marwood was in Maidstone for the execution of James Parnes who murdered six-year old William Crouch with an iron bar after the child's mother failed to keep an appointment with him. After Parnes committed the crime, he walked to the police station and confessed but this did not help him. All through his trial he prayed for forgiveness and on the gallows he was full of remorse praying along with the Chaplain in a loud voice.

On August 14th, Marwood was in Liverpool to execute two people. The first person was William Fish who murdered Emily Holland, a seven-year old girl whose body he dismembered. The second person executed on that day was Richard Thompson.

The following report came from the Liverpool Echo:

"At just after 4pm on the afternoon of March 27th, Emily Holland aged seven years-of-age, disappeared as she walked down Birley Street, Blackburn, after telling a friend she was going to fetch some tobacco for an adult. Emily was never seen again after that. At the end of a two-day search police found her legs and her torso, minus the head and arms, in a field. The torso revealed she had been violently raped, her throat had been cut and she had been dismembered. The body parts were wrapped in old copies of the Preston Herald. Two weeks later Robert Taylor, a tramp, was arrested after local children said he had been talking to them. Suspicion centred on a shopkeeper named William Fish who traded in Moss Street, near Birley Street. Police investigated and found copies of the Preston Herald in a corner of his shop which had issues missing corresponding exactly with those found wrapped round Emily's body parts. A local man offered the use of his bloodhound to help find the child's head and arms and some of her clothing. The dog was taken to Fish's shop where it began barking determinedly at the fireplace. Police looked up the chimney and found bloody copies of the Manchester Courier wrapped around the rest of Emily's body parts. A lynch party had gathered outside the shop and Fish had to be smuggled out the back way to the police station. The tramp was released, and Fish was hanged on Monday, August 14th, 1876, at Kirkdale Prison, Liverpool, alongside Richard Thompson, who had murdered John Bundell, from Liverpool."

Birley Street was to feature again in Blackburn's dark history over seventy years later, when child killer Peter

Griffiths was arrested outside his house on the same street.

On August 21st, Marwood was at Armagh, Ireland for the execution of Steven McKeown who murdered Mary McShane. Several years earlier her father had been murdered and McKeown was suspected of being responsible for that crime but had fled to America before he could be arrested. When McKeown returned to Armagh from America, Miss McShane took him to court after he had made repeated threats to her life when she spurned his advances. He was bound over to keep the peace and ordered to stay away from her. On Sunday April 23rd, he followed her into a field and brutally beat her about the head with a large stone. He was immediately arrested and at his trial was sentenced to death by Mr Justice Fitzgerald.

Marwood was at Cork, Ireland on August 25th, for the double execution of Christos Emmanuel Bombos, a mutineer and murderer aboard the ship 'Caswell,' and a sixty-three year old Fenian named Thomas Crowe.

From the synopsis of the book 'The Riddle of the Caswell Mutiny' by Seamus Breathnach, is this passage:

"In December, 1875 Captain George 'Bully' Best found himself in Buenos Aires without a crew and without a cargo. His men had for the most part deserted him. Before making his way to Antofogasta, where he loaded up with Saltpetre, he recruited 'a mixed crew' of Greeks and British. The British refused to sail with the Greeks, and rather than allow them onshore to see the British Consul, Captain Best beat them and put them in irons. Even before the Caswell sailed for Queenstown on

January 1, 1876, an Irishman and a German jumped ship and were never heard of again. Obvious tensions might lead one to expect a British mutiny. And perhaps this might have happened had not the Greeks beaten them to it. For some unexplained reason the Greeks, under the influence of 'Big George' Peno, mutinied and killed the Captain, the first and second mates, and the black Welsh steward. All four bodies were lashed to an anchor and thrown overboard. By February two of the mutineers, the brothers Pistoria, escaped by boat up the river Plate to Buenos Aires. The remainder drifted under Greek command until March 11th when the British counter mutinied and killed two of their captors. A third mutineer was brought back to Queenstown to be tried for 'Murder on the High Seas.' Young Christos Emmanuel Bombos found himself imprisoned with a sixty three year old Fenian named Thomas Crowe.

Both men provided the spectacle of a 'double hanging' in Cork's male prison. A full eyewitness account was given of the executions, which happen to be one of the most striking events in nineteenth century." Three years later one of the escaped mutineers was arrested in Monte Video and a second trial was staged in Cork and he was hanged. Of the sixteen persons who set out from Buenos Aires: two jumped ship; four were murdered in the mutiny; two were murdered in the counter-mutiny; six returned to tell the tale.

The second person Marwood executed August 25th, was Thomas Crowe who murdered John Hyland, a cart driver for the land agent Nat Buckley. After collecting a large amount of money from a client Buckley needed a police escort to take the money to the bank. As they were passing a wood, the cart was ambushed and John Hyland was shot and Crowe was arrested.

A local newspaper carried this report:

"Sixty three year old Thomas Crowe was found guilty of the murder of John Hyland, a driver who worked for a land agent called Nat Buckley, in Tipperary. Buckley was returning after collecting a large amount of money when the cart he was travelling in was ambushed as he passed a wood. The police who were escorting the agent caught one of the men, but he was left unattended when two others opened fire at the cart. During the fight, someone shot Hyland. When Crowe was arrested, he contested he was innocent and that he was the first man they had detained and that another man had the gun, not him but the police proved otherwise."

On August 29th, Marwood was in Newgate for the execution of John Ebblethrift who murdered his wife, Emma, with a knife. After drinking, Ebblethrift was known to be a violent man who regularly beat his wife. When he came home drunk one night, a neighbour offered Emma a bed for the night but she refused his offer. After a few moments of Ebblethrift arriving home the neighbour heard Emma screaming and went to investigate and found her dead on the floor of her bedroom. John was arrested and at his trial pleaded manslaughter due to jealousy but was convicted of murder and hanged.

Marwood was back at Newgate on December 11th, for the execution of Charles O'Donnell who beat his wife to death with a pair of fire tongs because she refused to give him money for drink.

A local newspaper carried this report:

"On Sunday, October 30th, fifty seven-year-old Charles O'Donnell, a labourer and former asylum inmate, visited some friends alone. During dinner he made certain statements that made them suspicious of why his wife Elizabeth hadn't accompanied him to their house.

They knew that the couple had been married for two years had been separated since he was released from the asylum and had only recently got back together and moved into a room in Chelsea. Next morning they notified the police who called at the room and found Mrs O'Donnell dead in bed. She had been battered to death with a pair of tongs that lay bloodstained on the floor. A neighbour in the flats told police that earlier in the week Mrs O'Donnell had given her some money to keep safe because her husband wanted to take it from her.

After O'Donnell's conviction his conduct in the prison was exemplary and he acknowledged the justice of his sentence. He complained that it had been brought about by a falsehood and perjury at his trial. Nevertheless, he declared that he forgave his enemies, and hoped that God would forgive them. It was said he slept well during the night preceding the execution and after breakfast he engaged in prayer with the chaplain who afterwards escorted him to the scaffold as the prison bell chimed eight o'clock. After the necessary preparations had been made, the drop fell and O'Donnell's life ended."

On the December 14th, Marwood was in Cambridge for the execution of Robert Browning who murdered a fifteen-year old prostitute, Emma Relfe. Browning was a twenty five year old tailor and former soldier. He was sentenced to death at Norwich Assizes on November 24th, for the murder of Emma Relfe, by cutting her throat. Despite her age the victim earned her living as a prostitute and had been living in a brothel for several weeks before the murder.

The report of the execution in the Times newspaper the next day was as follows:

"At 9.30pm on the night of Thursday 24th, August, 1876, Emma Relfe, aged 16, met up with Robert Browning, aged 25, near Four Lamps in Maids Causeway, Cambridge. But this was no young lovers' meeting. Emma was in the habit of selling her favours to anyone with a spare shilling. Browning was employed as a tailor in Covent Garden, off Mill Road. He lived with his parents and a brother and seemed to have been in the habit of spending his evenings drinking and seeking the company of young women of easy virtue, for which pleasures he was to pay a heavy price.

On the fateful evening he had worked with his brother to finish a pair of trousers for local trader Mr Ward, who had promised them five shillings if they finished on time. The Browning brothers completed the task and set off to spend the money on drink. At about 8.30pm Robert Browning parted company from his brother at the end of Bradmore Street and went home for supper. At this time he must have been brooding over something, for he ate very little and then told his mother he was going out. With perhaps a mother's instinct for his mood, she advised him not to, saying he had been out the three nights before. She advised him to go to bed, but instead Browning lit a candle and went and fetched a cutthroat razor, placing it in his overcoat pocket. He then left the house and went to a public house known as Canham's in Fair Street where he had more to drink. He walked from the pub to Four Lamps where he met not only Emma Relfe but another girl Browning later stated in evidence at his trial that he told them he didn't want two women. Emma's companion then left and Browning and Emma went onto Midsummer Common, in the area known as Butts Green, where he committed the crime. He had promised Emma a shilling to go with him but no money changed hands. Browning then walked to the Garrick Inn and had a glass of ale, his appearance and behaviour causing some notice among the clientele. He left after only a short time and was walking in the direction of home when he came upon PC Wheel who was in the area, having heard a dreadful shriek from the common. Upon seeing the constable, Browning promptly gave himself into custody, telling the officer that he had murdered a woman. At first he was not believed, so took PC Wheel to where his unfortunate victim lay dead. He handed the razor to the constable and showed him his bloodstained hands. A man named Southall, a traveller lodging at the Garrick Inn, assisted the constable with his prisoner, who was taken to the police station. Browning said at this time that he had killed Emma because she had robbed him of a shilling and he carried the razor with him as a matter of habit. However, Browning later made a written statement confessing the true reason for his dreadful crime. He wrote: I went out of the house intending to kill another girl called Bell, the girl who gave me a disease. Clearly,

Emma Relfe was not that girl and was merely an unfortunate substitute target for Browning's resentment. Emma's body had been taken to the Fort St George public house on Midsummer Common and it was there that the inquest was held on August 25th, 1876. The coroner's jury returned a verdict that her death was as a result of wilful murder by Robert Browning."

On August 29th, Browning was brought before the Mayor of the borough of Cambridge and other magistrates and committed for trial before Mr Justice Lush, to be held at Norwich on November 29th, 1876. At his trial Browning made little effort to defend himself and seemed resigned to his fate. He was sentenced to death with a recommendation of clemency from the jury 'on behalf of his youth.' The judge held out little hope of the prisoner's life being spared. Browning was taken to Cambridge borough gaol from Norwich gaol, where he awaited his trial. Dr Briscoe, Inspector of Prisons, who had been sent by the Home Office, saw him. Browning was interviewed at length to see if there was any reason why he should not be executed. Dr Biscoe's report was sent to the Home Secretary, who replied that he could not see any circumstances that would justify his interference with the due course of law. At a few minutes before 8.0am on December 14th, 1876, Browning was taken to the scaffold crying and sobbing. Marwood had adapted the apparatus by having a pit three feet deep dug beneath it. He had allowed a drop of six feet ten inches, on account of Browning being of light stature. In a few minutes the unhappy man ceased to live."

On November 29th, 1876, Marwood wrote a letter to the Governor of the Castle, in Lincoln.

Dear Sir,

"Please this is to inform you that i have received your kind letter this morning in regard to a prisoner under the sentence of death at the Castle the time appointed for the execution to take place the 18th Day of December i will engage with you to execute the prisoner at the time you have appointed: will arrive at Lincoln on Saturday the 16th Day of December i shall go direct to the Black Boy Inn near the Castle you may depend on me to be at Lincoln at the time appointed Sir Please i return to you many thanks for your great kindness to me i shall always be at your services when wanted Sir After the execution is over i shall go by the first train i can for London to execute a prisoner at Horsemonger Lane Prison on Tuesday morning the 19th all well. Sir I remain your humble servant. Please i have sent you 2 of my cards."

Since there is no record of an execution ever taking place on that day or the date mentioned at Lincoln in the letter, it is assumed that the prisoner was reprieved.

On December 19th, Marwood was at Surrey County Gaol (Horsemonger's Lane) for the execution of Silas Barlow who murdered Ellen Slopper and her child.

Silas Barlow was found guilty of the double murder of his former sweetheart Ellen Slopper and their young child, at Battersea on September 11th. They had lived together until she left him and moved to lodgings. He visited her twice at her new address and each time they had a meal together she felt sick after he left. Eventually she died, and the next day Barlow took custody of the child saying that his cousin would look after it. The child's body was later found floating in a Battersea reservoir. The body was identified, and when examined was found to have been poisoned with strychnine. Barlow was arrested and charged with murder after a search of his home produced bottles of the poison. The contents of Miss Slopper's stomach were then analysed and were found to contain poison. Barlow denied killing the woman but later admitted that he had killed the child.

After the execution Marwood caught the first train to Leicester for the execution of John Green the next day. John Green, a painter and decorator, shot dead his wife at their home at Leicester on August 21st, 1876. They had nine children. They had lived unhappily together due to Green being an alcoholic. On the day of the murder he told a colleague as they clocked off work that this would be his last day. Immediately after arriving home he walked into the house and shot his wife in the neck. She died in hospital later that night. The prosecution easily proved that it was premeditated murder and Green was convicted and hanged.

On December 21st, Marwood was in Manchester for the execution of William Flanagan who murdered Margaret Dockerty in her bed by cutting her throat. After living together as man and wife Flanagan decided to take Margaret to the racecourse where he worked as a gambler. After having a good day they returned home quite drunk and Flanagan went to lie down. When he got up he saw Margaret talking to one of the lodgers in the kitchen. Seeing them together he slapped Margaret's the face and ordered her to go to their room. In the morning Margaret did not show for breakfast and Flanagan said she was having a lie in. Their landlady went into the bedroom, saw that Margaret was dead in her bed and called the police. Flanagan was arrested and sent for trial. He pleaded insanity but was found guilty as charged. Whilst in custody he attempted suicide by cutting his throat.

An appeal was sent to the Home Secretary on the grounds of insanity but it was rejected. On the day of his execution Flanagan stepped firmly under the beam of the scaffold, and after casting a quick glance at the spectators, closed his eyes and submitted himself to the hangman. He did not appear to realize his position until the cap was drawn over his face when he fervently repeated the response "Lord have mercy upon me." Whilst his lips were moving the bolt was drawn and it was all over. The drop given by Marwood was over six feet long and he died instantaneously.

Chapter Six –
Executions 1877

During 1877, Marwood carried out twenty-one executions, the first one being at Horsemonger's Lane. The person he went to execute was Isaac Marks aged twenty-three-years. Isaac Marks was a Jewish antique dealer who shot Frederick Bernard seven times outside a shop in Lambeth.

A report in Times newspaper states:

"In the spring of 1874, Isaac Marks, a Jewish antique dealer, began to court Caroline Bernard and later, as the relationship flourished, he proposed marriage. Frederick Bernard, father of thirteen children and a fellow Jew, checked out his prospective son-in-law and gave his blessing to their engagement. All went well until the summer of 1876, when Marks' house was destroyed by fire. Bernard helped Marks to make the insurance claim and later presented him with a hefty bill for his services,

Marks was so angry at being asked to pay what he considered an unreasonable amount that he broke off the engagement. This caused great animosity between the two men. On the afternoon of October 24th, Marks waited outside a shop in Lambeth and as Bernard emerged he fired seven shots at him, killing him instantly. Marks was immediately detained by a member of the public and held until the police arrived. A shopkeeper testified that he had sold a gun to Marks only an hour before the crime, effectively ruining the defence of non-premeditated murder. Marks' counsel claimed that he was insane; he was known in his family as 'Mad Marks' and both his parents had died in an asylum. He was executed at Horsemonger Lane on January 2nd, 1877, aged twenty-three."

It was March 12th, before Marwood had another two executions to perform and for these he had to travel to Reading.

The first to be executed was Henry Tidbury and the second was Francis George Tidbury. Their crime was the murders of PC Shorter and Inspector Drewatt, members of the Berkshire Constabulary, after a poaching had taken place.

The Times report the next day is as follows:

"The two men convicted before Mr Justice Lindley at the Berkshire Assizes were executed yesterday morning in the grounds of Reading Gaol, in the presence of the prison officials and a few reporters.

The father and mother of the culprits visited them on the Saturday, with other members of the family. On

Sunday the culprits attended Divine Service in the gaol chapel, and were visited in their cells afterwards by the chaplain which lasted until ten o'clock at night then they went to bed. In the morning the day of the execution they rose at seven o'clock and at a quarter before eight o'clock were handed over to Marwood in the waiting room. The procession then formed and they were marched through the principle part of the gaol to the outer grounds, where they were pinioned. On reaching the final place of execution preparations were soon completed and the fatal bolt was drawn and the culprits died instantaneously without pain or struggle. The black flag was then hoisted and the crowd outside soon dispersed. After the inquest the bodies were buried near the western wall of the gaol.

Before the execution both prisoners wrote formal confessions of their guilt, copies of which were handed to the reporters after the execution had taken place. From these statements it appears that the constables were murdered in an attempt to apprehend the Tisbury's for poaching with their guns and were returning with two pheasants when Drewatt approached. As Inspector Drewatt was coming towards the poachers Henry fired and shot him. Police constable Shorter then approached and Francis shot at him but missed. The constable ran back down the lane in the direction of Hungerford, but the Tisbury's pursued him and battered him to death. They returned to Inspector Drewatt, who was not dead and expected them to spare him. However, they beat him about the head with their guns until he died."

On March 26th, Marwood was in Lincoln for the execution of William Clarke who murdered gamekeeper

Henry Walker. William Clarke, alias Slenderman, was sentenced to death at Lincoln Assizes on March 8th, 1877, for the murder in February of Henry Walker, a gamekeeper at Norton Disney. Clarke was arrested at Lowestoft and at his trial tried to prove he was with two friends at the time of the murder in Lowestoft. The prosecution proved otherwise.

A newspaper report from the Times of his execution dated March 29th, 1877, states:

"William Clarke was executed within the walls of Lincoln Castle at 9 o'clock. Since the prisoners condemnation he has paid ever attention to the ministrations of the prison chaplain, and was fully prepared to meet his doom. He was visited on Friday by several relatives. On the day of the execution he rose at seven o'clock and wrote a letter and at seven thirty received Sacrament. He was pinioned in his cell and led out to the place of execution from a side door of the prison. He walked without support but was ashy pale.

He ascended the steps firmly and as his legs were being strapped uttered the words 'Lord have mercy on my soul' Marwood quickly placed the cap over his head, adjusted the rope, and the drop fell with a heavy thud. The culprit appeared to die almost instantly, with only a slight movement in his legs being visible. The drop given was a little over five feet. In the late afternoon an inquest was held on the body.

This was Lincoln Castle's last execution."

Immediately after the execution Marwood left for Manchester Strangeways Prison where the next day he had to execute John McKenna. The police knew John McKenna as a drunkard. For committing assaults, he had been in court several times but on the evening of February 24th, 1877, he murdered his wife.

The following report was in the Manchester Guardian:

"McKenna, a Rochdale plasterer, was convicted of the murder of his wife, in what the prosecution claimed were pure unmitigated, brutal circumstances. Annie McKenna was the same age as her husband; they had been married for several years and had two children. They did not have a happy marriage on account of John's drunkenness, which often ended in violence against his pretty wife. On February 24th, McKenna and his heavily pregnant wife visited their neighbour, Mrs Higgins. John McKenna sent his wife out on more than one occasion to fetch ale before they went home in the evening. Later, Annie McKenna returned to Mrs Higgins home to seek refuge from her husband's threatening behaviour. McKenna, who had become drunk, went over to the Higgins house and demanded to see his wife. Mrs Higgins, who was quite used to shielding the unfortunate wife, told McKenna to go away and offered to buy him a quart of ale. McKenna refused, pushed his way inside and dragged his wife home by the hair. Fearing for her safety, Mrs Higgins rushed over to the McKenna house and saw through a window that McKenna was beating and kicking his wife. Mrs Higgins watched him repeatedly bang Annie's head against the floor before calling for another neighbour, Henry Dunn, to intervene. Dunn and McKenna quarrelled and fought outside the house whilst a mortally wounded Annie McKenna was treated inside. After twenty minutes of trading punches with Dunn, McKenna forced his way back into his house, lifted his wife's head on the pillow and started punching her about the face. She died soon after, by which time McKenna had fled. He was soon located in Liverpool and caught just before he boarded the boat for Ireland he was brought back to Manchester to await his fate, which came on March 27th."

Marwood had only one day at home before he was off on his travels again. His next execution took place in Chester on April 2nd. The person he executed was James Bannister who murdered his wife at their home. Bannister was convicted of the brutal and unprovoked murder of his wife at their home on Russell Street, in Hyde, Manchester. Early in the morning of December 15th, 1876, a Mr and Mrs Grayson, who lodged in the same house as Bannister and his wife, were awakened by moaning coming from across the corridor. They saw a light on and heard the sound of a blow being struck. Grayson ran into the room and found Mrs Bannister lying on the bed with her head bashed in. Her husband was lying beside her with a self-inflicted throat wound. They were both taken to hospital where she died the next day but Bannister recovered. Mr Justice Lush at Chester Assizes sentenced him to death.

Marwood's next execution took place at Warwick on April 17th, 1877. The condemned man was Frederick Edwin Baker who murdered Mary Saunders. Because Mary would not go out with him, Baker became jealous of any man she went with. He was heard to say on many occasions that if she did not go out with him, no other man would go out with her. After he killed her he was arrested and brought before the Assizes and sentenced to death by hanging.

Shortly after this execution William Marwood found time to buy some properties from Mr John Hall of Bucknall. They consisted of a freehold property called 'Pringle' and six cottages. The occupiers of the cottages at that time were Joseph Fletcher, William Appewhite, Joseph Hall, George Coupland, John Hall and John Young. After the sale they paid their rent to Marwood.

Two months later on July 31st, Marwood was engaged to carry out another execution at Leicester. The person he had to execute was John Henry Starkey who had murdered his wife. Starkey, a coachman and habitual criminal with a string of convictions under a number of aliases, was convicted of the murder of his wife. He married her at the beginning of the year but within weeks he had started seeing another woman. On April 4th, his wife taxed him about the affair. This angered him so much that he attacked her and her screams alerted the neighbours. At 8am the next morning, Starkey went to work and told a friend that he feared his wife had committed suicide. By 9am the body had been discovered with the head almost severed. Starkey was arrested and although there were bloodstains on his clothes he claimed he was innocent and that their lodger had killed his wife. He confessed to Marwood before he was hanged on July 31st, 1877.

Marwood's next execution took place on August 13th, in Chester. The condemned man was twenty–three year old Henry Leigh who murdered eight-year old Alice Hatton. The next day Marwood was at Horsemonger's

Lane (Surrey County Gaol) for the execution of Caleb Smith who had murdered Elizabeth Osborne. This was the last execution ever to take place in this gaol as it closed in 1878 and was demolished in 1881.

On April 14th, at their home in Croydon, thirty-eight year old Caleb Smith and his common-law wife, Emma Elizabeth Osborne, had another in a long series of drunken quarrels during which she slapped his face. In a rage Smith pulled out his razor and cut Emma's throat before turning the blade on himself. He was tried at the Central Criminal Court on July 24th, 1877, and pleaded manslaughter through provocation. The jury found him guilty and he was executed on August 14th, 1877.

Marwood had to carry out two executions at Liverpool's Kirkdale Gaol on August 21st. The condemned were John Golding who murdered Daniel Lord and Patrick McGovern who murdered John Campbell. John Golding and Daniel Lord were friends and lived within a few streets of each other at Edge Hill. On July 16th, they had a quarrel which ended with Golding beating Lord about the head with a poker. Three days later Lord, died from his injuries. Mr Justice Hawkins at Liverpool Assizes sentenced Golding to death although the jury recommended mercy.

Patrick McGovern was a labourer who was convicted of the murder of John Campbell on July 23rd, 1877. Campbell was a Liverpool butcher who happened to be passing by when McGovern and his wife were having an argument on their doorstep. At a request from Mrs McGovern, Campbell tried to persuade McGovern to let his wife into the house. McGovern responded by stabbing Campbell to death with a carving knife.

It was October 21st, before Marwood carried out another execution, this time at Newgate. The condemned on this occasion was John Lynch who murdered his wife by cutting her throat. John Lynch lived with his wife for nine years in Brighton. They had four children, the youngest dying in June 1877, which was very upsetting for the family. After the funeral John's wife went to stay with her aunt, Alice Carmody, in London, taking the children with her. On July 1st, her husband followed and after the journey he went to lie down in her bed, as she had gone for a walk with her aunt. When they returned John's wife went with their daughter to wake him. He became violent and started beating her. Alice's husband called the police and had him put out of the house. On July 4th, John bought a razor from a shop in the city and sent a message to his wife to meet him to talk things over. The meeting took place the following day. After taking her for a few drinks in various public houses she told him "I've had enough. I'm not coming home with you. I might see you sometime tomorrow, though." They had been married for only five years, but lately Lynch had turned to beating her. She had already taken out a summons against him for common assault but it hadn't seemed to make any difference. Lynch suddenly whipped out a razor and cut her throat. She staggered a few yards and then collapsed and died on the pavement.

"Now I'm satisfied," Lynch was heard to say. The police came and charged with him murder.

At his trial a letter was produced dated August 4th. It was a summons to appear at court for an assault on his wife. This was proved to be the reason for purchasing the razor and murdering his wife.

On November 12th, Marwood was back at Newgate for the execution of Thomas Benjamin Pratt who murdered Elizabeth Francis Rockington. Pratt was sentenced to death at the Central Criminal Court on October 25th, 1877, for the murder of Elizabeth, with whom he lived. She had threatened to leave if he didn't curb his violent habits and although he repeatedly vowed he would, he failed to keep his promise. Elizabeth eventually left him but Pratt tracked her down and stabbed her to death. He was brought to court and sentenced to death for the crime he had committed.

On November 19th, Marwood was in Exeter for the execution of William Hassell who had murdered his wife.

On October 8th, Hassell, a Barnstable butcher, returned home drunk and stabbed his wife three times with a pig-knife while she was breast-feeding their baby. They had repeatedly quarrelled and he had become dismayed at their unhappy life. Hassell refused legal aid and pleaded guilty at his trial, although a petition for a reprieve was organised on the strength that he was drunk when he committed the crime. According to the local newspaper Hassell walked to the scaffold with a firm step but cried bitterly before he was hanged.

From Exeter Marwood went to Norwich Castle to execute Henry Marsh who had murdered Thomas Mays and Henry Bidwell. Marsh and Bidwell worked together in a forge at Wymondham, Norfolk which was owned by Thomas Mays. During the summer both men learned that they were to lose their jobs as Mays was retiring and selling the business. Marsh was particularly upset as he had been employed at the forge for thirty-seven years and while out on an errand he called at a pub and had several drinks. When he returned to work he got into a row with Bidwell and in a rage beat him to death with a heavy iron bar. A servant girl at the house saw the attack and rushed to tell the elderly owner. When Mays entered the forge, Marsh turned on him and declared: "I might as well swing for two as for one," and beat the old man to death. He was executed on November 20th, 1877.

On November 21st, Marwood was at Nottingham to execute Thomas Grey who had murdered Ann Mellor. Mr Justice Hawkins sentenced Grey to death on October 31st, at the Nottinghamshire Assizes for the murder of Ann at Carcolston in August.

Ann lived with her mother and brother in a village shop and was engaged to a man from Middlesborough named Holt, who at the time of the crime was staying with them. Early in the morning of August 20th, Thomas Grey entered the shop. He had repeatedly tried to court Ann but she had shown no interest in him, and the appearance of Holt had fuelled him in a jealous passion. Finding her alone in the shop, he tried to force his advances on her. When she pushed him away, he pulled a knife out of his pocket and cut her throat repeatedly.

The Nottingham Journal dated November 21st, 1877, states:

"The man Thomas Grey who will be hanged this morning presents none of those traits which are generally observed in the typical murderer. By far the larger portion of his life has been passed in the village of Car Colston with his parents, who are simple village folk, his father getting his living from the produce of a small cottage farm. The mans life then, has been passed amidst harmless pursuits, surrounded by few temptations; and as far as we know his life has not been darkened by the shadow of any previous crime or misdemeanour which has brought him under the eye of the law. He seems, however, to have been anything but a pleasant fellow in the village; he was habitually taciturn, frequently morose and bad tempered, and a dangerous man to anger."

On November 23rd, Marwood was to officiate at Dolgelly's last execution. The condemned person was Cadwallader Jones who murdered his girlfriend, Sarah Hughes. Jones was sentenced to death for the murder of thirty-six year old Sarah in June. They began an affair and when Jones fell out of love with his prim and proper wife, he went to live with Sarah Hughes. She disappeared on June 2nd, and no trace of her was found until parts of her body were later washed up from a river. Police ascertained the body was Sarah Hughes and investigations led them to Jones. He confessed that he had killed Sarah by striking her with a large stone after she told him she was pregnant and began to pester him for money. He showed the police where he had buried the remains of her body.

A petition, signed by 10,000 persons, was forwarded to the Home Secretary who declined to interfere with the course of the law. Jones walked firmly to the drop, praying fervently died without a struggle. He was hanged on a scaffold borrowed from Chester Prison.

The last execution of 1877 was a triple execution that took place at Leicester on November 27th. Marwood's convicts were James Satchell, John Swift and John Upton who had murdered Joseph Tugby by beating and kicking him to death.

The Leicester Daily Mercury states:

"The unfortunate victims of Marwood were employed at Ellistown Colliery, near Coalville when the murder took place on the morning of September 1st, 1877; Swift and Satchell as colliers and Upton as banksman. The last named prisoner was tried and convicted under an assumed name. His native village was Newbury, Staffordshire and had had previous convictions against him. Only a fortnight before the participation in the crime, he, in the company with Satchell obtained employment at the colliery. Satchell and Swift both had visits from friends and relatives but Upton only received a letter from his.

The executioner, Marwood, arrived in Leicester soon after nine o'clock on Sunday morning, and, quietly and unrecognised, proceeded to the County Gaol, where he took up his quarters. Arrangements were immediately made for the erection of the scaffold, the same which had been used for the execution of Starkey whom he executed on the 31st July, and which had been lent by the county authorities. It had to be strengthened, and that work was entrusted to Messrs Herbert.

So far as can be ascertained by the Press, the extreme height of the scaffold is seven feet, and from the cross beams three chains were suspended through which the ropes were to be placed. Underneath the drop there was probably a space of fifteen feet. Owing to the refusal to admit the Press we are unable to say the length of the drops, but it may generally be taken that the ropes varied in lengths according to the heights and weights of the victims.

The meals of Marwood have been supplied by Mr. T. Andrews of the Turks Head Inn, which immediately faces the gaol, and the executioner has not been outside the gaol since his arrival. About midnight on Monday the arrangements for the burials of the unfortunate men were completed, they are to be buried on the left hand side of the Governors house within the precincts of the gaol.

THE MORNING OF THE EXECUTION.

After a heavy night's rain, which did not cease until about half past one, there came on a heavy mist and drizzling rain, at half past five morning broke and the stars shone brightly, and everything seemed peaceful and calm. Dark as it was the approaches to the County Gaol were surrounded by people. The number was not large, but there were many curious and morbid persons assembled. At twenty minutes to eight o'clock the bell of Trinity Church was tolled, and five minutes later a man was seen to ascend the left turret by a ladder, making preparations for the hoisting of the black flag. A shudder ran through the crowd in anticipation of the horrible scene to follow within the walls so shortly afterwards and the very slight conversation carried on was hushed.

As the clock marked the hour when the unfortunate men were led out to execution, the mournful tolling of the passing bell, rang out dolefully in the cold air. Those who were possessed with any humane feeling uttered a silent prayer for the souls of those who were to pass away. At eight o'clock precisely, the men who had been pinioned went to their execution, headed by the Rev James and those officials concerned. The men, we were informed, went to their fate with perfect resignation, and they were launched into eternity, dying without a struggle. The crowd assembled outside the gaol heard the thud occasioned by the fall of the drop, distinctly. At exactly five minutes past eight the black flag was run up, and the crowd, which had increased by the time of the execution, gradually dispersed."

Chapter Seven – Executions 1878

During the years 1878 to 1883, Marwood wrote ten letters to the authorities applying for the post of assistant at hangings in other parts of the country.

In January 1878, the Government Authorities told Marwood that he had to stop using his own ropes and instead use the official ones made by Messrs Edgington and Co., Long Lane, London. They were made from white Italian hemp, two and a half inches in circumference with four strands, which had a metal ring and a leather washer fitted to stop it slipping.

The first execution of 1878 took place on February 4th, at Manchester Strangeways Prison. The person Marwood had to execute was George Piggott who murdered Florence Galloway. In 1876 Piggott, a married man with two small children left his wife after seducing Florence, a young domestic servant. He set up home with this lover in Birmingham.

Florence was only seventeen and she was head over heels in love with him. She was a domestic servant in a Manchester suburb and he, George Piggott, drove the tram she caught when making visits to her mother in Lower Broughton, Salford. George never talked about marriage, and that perplexed Florence. One day he told her: "I'm giving up my job and trying my luck in Birmingham." Florence was flabbergasted.

"What about me?" she demanded to know. "What about us?"

Piggott gave her a kiss.

"Of course I want you to come, too," he said.

Although he told her he couldn't really afford to marry her that moment, to her mother's shock and horror, Florence packed her bags and set off to Birmingham to live with George.

She was soon to discover that living with Piggott was not nearly as romantic as riding on his tram. He got drunk, beat her regularly and became very possessive. Florence was pregnant within a year.

Facing up to his terrible temper, she told him, "We'll have to get married now."

Piggott however, instead of creating a scene, burst into floods of tears.

"I can't marry you, luv," he sobbed. "I've already got a wife and three children."

Next morning Florence pawned a few items to buy a train ticket to Manchester and she went back to mother's house. Piggott moved back in with his wife, who forgave him for the affair. He took a job as a tram driver again.

Piggott was missing Florence and wanted to see her again. He guessed where Florence had gone and went to find her. For days he waited outside her mother's house in Lawn Street but she refused to come out. Finally he sent her mother a note, via a small boy, saying the note had come from a Mrs. Wilson, inviting her and her daughter round for tea. When Florence and her mother came out on to the street at the appointed hour, Piggott appeared and blocked their path.

"Go away to your poor wife and children!" yelled Mrs. Galloway.

Piggott tried to reason with her, and she began to scream.

When he said: "Won't you let me do anything for Florence?"

Mrs. Galloway shouted, "No! No!"

At this Piggott raised his hand to Florence's head and said quietly: "Take that."

A shocked Mrs. Galloway heard a deafening explosion and saw the flash from a pistol. She felt her daughter go limp in her arms. "Murder!" she screamed, as Piggott turned and fled.

Florence died two days later in hospital, having made a statement identifying her killer.

Piggott was tried at the Manchester Assizes in January 1878, where he claimed that he had no intention of shooting Florence. He had taken the gun out to shoot himself if she refused to come back and live with him. The jury refused the plea and he was sentenced to death and was hanged on Monday, February 4th, 1878, at Manchester Strangeways Prison. His last words on the scaffold were, "Lord Jesus, receive my soul." He was twenty-nine years old when the sentence was carried out.

On February 11th, 1878, Marwood was in Winchester for the execution of James Caffyn who murdered Maria Barber. Caffyn was an illiterate labourer who was charged with the murder of Maria at Ryde on the Isle of Wight. They had been living together in a house they shared with her father and his lover when, on Monday, November 27th, 1877, a neighbour heard screams and saw Maria covered in blood fleeing from the house. Another neighbour went inside to remonstrate with Caffyn and saw him put down an axe. Later that day Maria died. Caffyn fled to Portsmouth but was arrested. He claimed that the motive for the crime was her threat to leave him and therefore it was a case of manslaughter, caused by provocation. The jury refused to believe him and he was sentenced to death.

On February 12th, Marwood was in Liverpool for the execution of James Trickett who murdered his wife Mary.

This item came from the Liverpool Echo, which states:

"Mary has been permanently drunk for more than six months," James Trickett, 42, told the police as they gazed down at the dead body of his wife on Boxing Day, 1877.

"She fell down the stairs and banged her head."

The neighbours had a different view of how Mary, aged thirty-five had died. "They had non-stop rows," one of them said. "He was the one who was always drunk, and he was always beating her up, said another.

After further questioning Trickett, who was described as a bird-catcher and owner of a pet shop in Hopwood Street in the Vauxhall area of Liverpool, agreed there had been a scuffle. The post-mortem revealed more than a scuffle – there was a stab wound under Mary's left breast and extensive bruising all over her body.

Trickett pleaded guilty to manslaughter at his trial at Liverpool Assizes in January 1878, but was found guilty of murder.

The Home Office ignored the jury's recommendation for mercy and Trickett was hanged on Tuesday, February 12th, 1878, at Kirkdale Prison."

On February 13th, Marwood was in Nottingham Prison to execute John Brooks for the murder of Carolyn Woodhead.

Carolyn Woodhead, a married woman left her husband and roamed the country with John Brooks before settling in Nottingham. There she became homesick and returned to live with her mother. When John found out where Carolyn was living he went round to the house armed with a knife. When she answered the door he grabbed her and cut the poor girl's throat. He buried her at the bottom of the garden and then fled the scene. He was soon caught and was brought to trial. In December 1877, he was sentenced to death at the

Nottingham Assizes. He was executed on February 13th, 1878.

After a few weeks without any executions Marwood had some time at home with his wife. It was during this time that two visitors came to his shop and whilst one occupied his attention with animated conversation, the other, standing behind his friend, sketched William's likeness. They gave him a liberal fee, made a purchase or two and promised to call again in a fortnight. They kept their word and Marwood was very curious about who they were but remained in ignorance until some time later.

Journeying to London in the fulfilment of his duties, Marwood was startled to learn that his likeness was portrayed in the waxworks of Madame Tussaud. Marwood denied it, declaring that it could not be. However, on visiting the waxworks, Marwood had the pleasure or pain of looking at the handiwork of the two artists who had so cleverly deceived him.

On April 1st, Marwood was in Oxford for the execution of Henry Rowles who had murdered his fiancée Mary Allen.

On April 15th, Marwood was at York Castle for the execution of Vincent Knowles Walker who had murdered Lydia White.

A report from the local newspaper states:

"When a wife walks out, there's no knowing what might happen next. Ship's carpenter Vincent Walker was sure he knew what was happening when his wife left their matrimonial home in Hull. She had gone to live with her friend Mrs. Lydia White, and Walker was convinced that Mrs. White was encouraging her to sleep around. As rumours of Mrs. Walker's infidelities spread, Walker, 48, worked himself up into an enormous rage. First he bought an axe, announcing his intention to kill both women, before friends disarmed him. Two days later he brandished a sword in his local, and was again disarmed.

In February 1878, unable to contain himself any longer, he called on his wife at 37 Nile Street. Lydia White, the object of Walker's fury, opened the door and without a moment's thought he lunged at her with his knife, stabbing her thirty times. She fell dying on the doorstep.

Terrified by her friend's screams, Mrs. Walker fled from the house by the back door, which was as well, for Walker later told police he would have killed her too. He was caught fleeing down the road and brought back to the house, where he managed to break free and kick Mrs. White's dead body.

He was hanged on Monday, April 15th, 1878, at York Prison."

"It was a botched execution," stated the other local newspapers of the town, "with the prisoner writhing in agony on the end of the rope while he died from slow strangulation."

On May 31st, Marwood was in Edinburgh for the execution of Eugene Marie Chantrelle who murdered his wife Elizabeth. Eugene was a very intelligent man who wished to be a doctor in the early years but, before he could complete his studies, his father's business floundered and without funding Eugene had to withdraw. After spending some time in America he moved to Edinburgh where he became a teacher. He had a pupil named Elizabeth Dyer. They became attracted although she was only fifteen. He got her pregnant and the couple got married when she was seventeen and he was thirty-four. After a while Eugene took to drinking and visiting brothels. He had taken out an insurance policy the previous year on Elizabeth for one thousand pounds that included a clause for accidental death. Elizabeth knew she was in danger and told her parents of her fears. They refused to believe her.

On New Years Eve 1877, Eugene plied her with drink and poisoned her with opium. He tried to disguise the poisoning by making the death look like the result of a broken gas main in the bedroom. Traces of opium were found in vomit stains on his wife's nightgown and in her hair. Two doctors visited her at home and she was taken to hospital where she died. Chantrelle was arrested and charged after his flat and study at the school where he worked were searched. A substantial amount of poison was found.

At his trial in May 1878, his defence tried to prove that he was innocent of murder. His excuse was that his wife had committed suicide was thrown out of court and when he was found guilty, showed no remorse. An appeal was applied for but was turned down. Eugene Chantrelle was hanged at Calton Prison on May 31st, 1878. Right up to the moment of his execution he proclaimed he was innocent and showed no sign of repenting.

Marwood's next execution was at Chelmsford on July 29th, where he executed Charles Joseph Revell who killed his wife Hester. On July 30th, Marwood was at Durham where he executed Robert Vest for the murder of John Wallace. Robert Vest was a ship's steward who was convicted of the murder of William John Wallace, a pilot on the barge 'William Leckie', at Sunderland. The captain of the barge had cautioned Vest for being drunk on duty and Wallace had sided with the captain. Shortly afterwards, Wallace went to a closet where he was surprised by Vest who stabbed him in the throat and abdomen. Vest was detained on the barge until the police could take him into custody. Sentenced to death by Mr Justice Bagalley on July 14th, after a plea of insanity had failed, the jury did recommend mercy. Vest was executed on July 30th, 1878, in Durham.

Marwood's next execution took place at Nottingham on August 12th. The condemned man was Thomas Cholerton who had murdered Jane Smith.

Cholerton and Jane had lived together as man and wife until the end of May when she left him because of his ill treatment of her. She went to stay with a family called Lynch. At 7pm on June 6th, Cholerton went to the Lynch house and later he and Jane left together. At around 10pm that night, an old man heard screaming and when he went to investigate found Jane on the ground with Cholerton kneeling over her cutting her throat. The old man dragged him off and almost at once a police officer arrived at the scene. Before she died in the street, Jane pointed weakly at Cholerton, who then attempted to cut his own throat, pleading with the officer: "Let me kill myself." He was convicted at Nottinghamshire Assizes, before Mr Justice Hawkins on July 28th, and executed on August 12th, 1878.

On August 15th, Marwood was in the town of Bodmin to execute a female, Selina Wadge, who murdered her illegitimate son by drowning him. It was revealed at the trial that she was so poor she could not look after him properly and that she loved him so much she could not let him suffer by not having any food to give him. She was sorry for what happened.

There had been no other executions in Cornwall for sixteen years, and as this was the first since the abolition of public executions, there was a good deal of curiosity about the proceedings, but the curious were disappointed.

Wadge was resigned to her fate, and was seen sobbing as she approached the scaffold. It was reported that she died instantaneously and without a struggle. It is said that her ghost still haunts the prison and it tries to reach out to small children as they pass by.

On October 3rd, Marwood was at Cupar, Scotland for the execution of William McDonald who murdered his wife.

A report from the Fife post 1878 states:

"At Perth Circuit Court, William McDonald a fisherman from St. Andrews was convicted and sentenced to death for the murder of his wife on the 13th, June. Afterwards he tried to commit suicide but was revived by a doctor who was tempted to let him slip away for he knew he would surely hang for his crime.

At his trial after he recovered he declared himself innocent of the murder saying he had done it with the consent of his wife in a pact to end their miserable existence. The Judge had no option but to have him hanged within the Cupar prison grounds for the crime he had committed. After the hanging he was buried in front of the East door of the prison, but there is no mark to indicate the grave."

On October 8th, Marwood carried out Wandsworth's first execution. The condemned person was Thomas Smithers who murdered Amy Judge. Thirty-one year old Thomas Smithers and Amy Judge lived together at Battersea. On July 18th, he stabbed Amy to death in a jealous rage. Although Smithers admitted his guilt and expressed sorrow for the crime, Mr Justice Denman showed no leniency and passed the death sentence. On September 18th, Smithers fainted in the dock and needed to be carried from the courtroom. He was executed on October 8th, 1878, at Wandsworth House of Correction.

The November 12th, Marwood was in Northampton for the execution of John Patrick Byrne who murdered Qtr. Sgt. Griffiths.

On November 18th, Marwood was in Usk for the execution of Joseph Garcia who murdered five members of the Watkins family.

A report from a local newspaper states:

"On the morning of Wednesday July 17th, a young farm worker called at the house of forty-year-old William Watkins, at Llangilly, near Newport, to find out why he had failed to report for work. As he approached he noticed smoke coming from an upstairs window and entering the house he discovered the bodies of Watkins, his wife Elizabeth who was slightly older than her husband at forty four, and their three children: Charlotte aged eight, Frederick who was five, and Alice just four. Mr and Mrs Watkins had been stabbed to death while the children had been hacked to death with an axe, as they lay asleep. Their bed was then set alight. On the previous morning a Spanish sailor named Joseph Garcia had been released from Usk Prison after serving a nine-month sentence for house breaking. On the Wednesday night a mail cart driver witnessed him walking towards Newport, and offered him a lift, which Garcia refused. When the driver reached the town he read about the murder and reported the suspicious traveller to the police who set up observation points around the town. Garcia was spotted as he entered the town and police noticed that he had cuts, bruises, bloodstains and other obvious signs of a struggle. When searched he had in his pockets some items he hadn't been in possession of when released from prison. He spoke little English and protested his innocence through a Spanish counsel. He was executed on November 18th, 1878, at Usk. All the time he was in gaol he protested that he was innocent but said he was prepared to die if had done anything wrong. He did not sleep at all during the Sunday night prior to the execution. Marwood went to the prisoner at just before eight o'clock and he was pinioned, but was so weak from not eating anything he partially fainted and had to be held erect by the warders. He came round as he was lead out into the corridor and again protested that he was innocent. On the scaffold he again had to be supported by the prison warders whilst the rope was adjusted round his neck. A crucifix was placed in his hands which he kissed before the lever was pulled and he fell to his death which was apparently instantaneous."

On November 19th, Marwood was at Manchester Strangeways Prison for the execution of James McGowan who murdered his wife.

A report from the Bolton Evening News states:

"As a result of being a heavy drinker, fifty five year old McGowan, a Salford bleach worker, began to suffer delusions and became convinced that his nephew, whom he had taken a sudden and unexpected dislike to, was attempting to break into his house. He told his wife of the break in and, knowing it to be all in his head, she refused to help him. This caused him to grow angry and as a result he threw her to the ground. She climbed to her feet and they began to struggle, during which he hacked away at her throat with a pocketknife. She died and he collapsed in a drunken heap. When he recovered his senses he threw the knife away and reported the crime to the police.

At his trial his defence said that a doctor had seen him and he claimed he seemed to be suffering from 'homicidal mania' but the plea was rejected and he was executed on November 19th, 1878."

On November 25th, Marwood was to officiate at Huntingdon's last execution. He was there to execute Henry Gilbert who murdered his bastard son. Thirty-year old Henry Gilbert was an agricultural labourer sentenced to death by Mr Justice Hawkins at Cambridge

Assizes on November 6th, for the murder of his illegitimate child.

Gilbert lived with a woman called Colbert at Wailweston, near Huntingdon, and evidence showed that he had been repeatedly cruel to the child and at various times had kicked and beaten it. The child died as a result of being struck about the head as it lay in bed. Gilbert admitted the crime but claimed he never intended to commit murder. The jury recommended mercy for Gilbert but it was refused and he was executed on November 25th, 1878.

Chapter Eight – Executions 1879

In 1879 Marwood wrote a letter to a prison explaining how an execution takes place.

"Sir, in Replie to your Letter of this Day I will give you a Compleat Staitment for Executing a Prisoner

1 - Pinnion the Prisoner Round the Boadey and Arms Tight

2 - Bair the Neck.

3 - Take The Prisoner to the Drop

4 - Place the Prisoner Beneath the Beam to stand Direct under the Rope from the Top of the Beam

5 - Strap the Prisoners Leggs Tight

6 - Putt on the Cap

7 - Putt on the Rope Round the Neck Thite Let the Cap be Free from the Rope to hide the Face angine Dow in Frunt

8 - Executioner to go Direct Quick to the
Leaver Let Down the Trap Doors Quick
No Greas to be Putt on the Rope"

Sir I remain your humble servant.

On January 10th, 1879, Marwood was in Limerick, Ireland for the execution of Thomas Cunceen who murdered Hannah Hogan and her chid. Thomas Cunceen was sentenced to death at Cork Assizes on Friday, December 13th, 1878, for the murder of Hannah Hogan, with whom he lived, and their child, at Singland. Cunceen had led the woman and child to a lonely spot then battered them to death and concealed their bodies beneath a heap of manure. Found guilty, he was executed in Limerick on the January 10th, 1879.

On February 4th, 1879, Marwood was in Maidstone to execute Stephen Gambrill who had murdered Arthur Gillow. Twenty eight year old Gambrill was a farm labourer sentenced to death at Kent Assizes on January 14th, for the murder of Arthur Gillow aged twenty-four, the son of a gentleman farmer.

A report the Maidstone Journal states:

"The harvest was poor, bread had reached a crazy price, it was close to Christmas and the farm labourers were on strike. This was Kent in 1878, a county where hunger and hatred were poisoning the land. Farm vandalism caused by the strikers was rife, and the landowning gentry feared for their properties, if not their lives. Marauders had come at night to Gillow's Farm in Sandwich, leaving a trail of havoc behind them; as a result Arthur had volunteered to stay up through the night to keep guard. On the morning of December 5th, his body was discovered beaten to death in the grounds. Gambrill was suspected of the crime and charged when enough evidence was collected against him. He confessed in the condemned cell but maintained that he had only killed in self-defence. He was executed on February 4th, 1879, in Maidstone."

On February 10th, 1879, Marwood was in Worcester for the execution of Enoch Whiston who murdered Alfred Merredith.

An article in Berrows Journal, February 15th, 1879, states:

"The circumstances of the murder of Alfred Merredith by Enoch Whiston, at Woodside, near Dudley, in December, so lately reported, in connection with the trial at the Assizes.

It will be remembered that Merredith who was the clerk to Messrs Smith and Hill, of Brierley Hill Ironworks, went on 6th December to a bank in Dudley to cash a cheque, and received a sum of about £280. On leaving the bank he was watched from the window of a public house, by Whiston, who closely followed him across the fields and through Woodside, shot him in the head with a pistol loaded with slugs, and took from him the money.

Whiston was followed to the house of a young woman named Terry, with whom he had kept company, and to whom, just before the police arrived, he had given £25. Some time previously he told Terry that he was going to work in Shropshire and before leaving should bring her £25 which he had at home.

When he was apprehended the police found in the pocket of his coat the pistol which again had been loaded. When in custody at the police station he made certain statements as to where the rest of the stolen money could be found. Before and after committal to the Assizes, and during his trial, he manifested the greatest unconcern. His deafness might in some small degree have accounted for the want of attention to the conclusive evidence given against him. It was urged by counsel for the defence that his actions were not those of a man of sound mind, but the jury, after brief deliberation and without recommendation to mercy found him guilty, and the execution of Whiston, whose age was put down in the Assizes calendar as twenty-one was fixed for Monday Feb 10th.

The prison officials declined to give any information as to his demeanour whilst under sentence, but it was understood that he had became resigned to his fate, and had no expectation of a reprieve.

He was seen by some of his friends on the Wednesday and on Thursday by his mother and other relatives and the girl Terry who then took their final leave of him. Petitions were signed in the city and at Hart's Hill, near Dudley where the prisoner lived and worked and were presented to the Home Secretary. They set forth that for many years the prisoner had been known by his fellow workmen and others to be of weak intellect, and prayed that on the ground that he was not of sound mind, the extreme penalty of the law might not be carried out.

On Wednesday, the 5th, inst, two medical men from London, receiving their instructions from the Home Office, saw the condemned man, and reported their opinion to the Home Secretary, then on Sunday a communication was received at the prison that after a full enquiry and careful consideration of the circumstances, he has failed to discover any sufficient grounds to justify him advising Her Majesty to interfere with the due course of the law.

The prisoner wrote to his friends, acknowledging the justice of the sentence passed upon him, and saying he was content to die. He attended the daily service in the chapel, and was present on Sunday, when the Sacrament was administered to him. The chaplain of the prison, the Rev G. C. Salt, frequently saw him, and was with him on Monday morning.

Shortly before eight o'clock the executioner Marwood, who had been at the prison since Saturday went to his cell, where Whiston was pinioned. On the way from the cell to the place of execution – the centre of the central yard of the prison – Whiston was very calm, not needing any support from the warders. In consequence of directions given by the High Sheriff no representatives of the press were present. The gallows was borrowed from Northampton, it being found that the one previously used in Worcester Prison could not be made available without great alteration. A pit was made as to allow a drop of eight feet six inches.

The prisoner walked up the half a dozen steps to the scaffold without assistance, and was firm whilst the cap was drawn over his face and the noose adjusted. Just as the hour of eight struck the drop fell. Death was instantaneous there being no sign of a struggle.

Five or six hundred persons assembled outside the prison and listened to the tolling of the bell (which commenced at a quarter to eight) and watched for the appearance of the black flag. A warder was stationed over the principle entrance to the prison, and when the signal was given from the place of execution (just as the Cathedral clock finished striking), the flag, which had a few minutes previously been run up to the top of the staff, was unfolded.

The body was taken down at nine o'clock, and at twelve an inquest was carried out in the gaol. After the body had been inspected, the jury assembled in the Visiting Justices' room then the body was subsequently buried near the boundary wall on the north side of the prison.

This was the second private execution in Worcester Prison. The previous one was on August 12th, 1872, when Charles Holmes was hanged for the murder of his wife at Eachway, near Bromsgrove."

Marwood's next execution took place at Lancaster Castle on February 11th, 1879. The condemned person he had to execute was William McGuiness who had murdered his wife. On Friday October 19th, McGuiness returned to his home at Barrow from his job as a labourer on a building site at Carnforth railway station. He had threatened a workmate that he'd commit murder before leaving Barrow for his native Ireland. Later that night a neighbour heard a disturbance at the house but paid no heed to it. A week later the next-door neighbour, while hanging out washing, climbed onto a fence and looked through Mrs Ann McGuiness's window and saw her body on the floor. When the body was examined, it was discovered she had been kicked to death. McGuiness was traced to Dublin after a magazine carried a description of the crime and the wanted man; he was arrested and brought back to face trial. Sentenced to death by Mr Justice Thesiger at Lancaster Assizes, he was executed on February 11th, 1879.

On February 25th, 1879, Marwood's next execution was at Leeds Armlet Prison, where he dispatched Charles Frederick Peace, for the murders of PC Cock and Arthur Dyson. This was one of Marwood's most famous executions.

This report came from the Bolton Evening News:

"Charles Peace was a notorious cat burglar and murderer who evaded arrest for over twenty years. He was a master of disguise, and often carried his housebreaking tools inside an old violin case, an instrument on which he was very proficient.

In 1877 while living at Banner Cross Terrace, Sheffield, he began an affair with a neighbour, Mrs Katherine Dyson. Although she was a willing instigator of the relationship, she soon decided that she wanted no further part of it and tried to be rid of him. Eventually Peace took the hint and left the area. He moved to Manchester and shot dead a policeman, PC Nicholas Cock, but the crime was attributed to a young Irishman,

William Habron, who was convicted and sentenced to death which was later commuted to life imprisonment on account of his young age. During the summer, Peace decided to return to Sheffield where he again started chasing after Mrs Dyson. One night her husband caught him with her and Peace shot him dead. He fled to London and set himself up with a new name but was soon in trouble again, he was convicted at Leeds Assizes and sentenced to death. William Marwood executed him after he confessed to the murder of PC Cock at the Assizes, which resulted in the release of William Habron from prison and eight hundred pounds compensation for his time in gaol.

On February 25th, 1879, the records from the time indicated it was a bitterly cold day when Charles Peace went to the gallows and he was convinced that he had been forgiven for his sins. At his last meeting with his wife, Hannah, he gave her a funeral card that read: "In Memory of Charles Peace who was executed in Armlet Prison, Leeds on Tuesday February 25th, 1879, Aged 47."

The full story of the case and his execution can be found in 'A Book of Remarkable Criminals' by H. B. Irving 1818.

This is the report of the execution is taken from the Times newspaper:

"Charles Peace was yesterday executed within the precincts of Armley Gaol, Leeds, for the murder of Mr Arthur Dyson.

Peace had a final interview with his relatives the previous day, and spent some time with them in earnest prayer. Peace was now thoroughly worn out by the excitements he had passed through and the chaplain left him to seek 'a few hours' sleep.

Peace slept soundly until a quarter to 6, and an hour later he partook very heartily of a breakfast which consisted of toast, bacon, eggs and tea.

The gallows was erected at the western side of the prison, and in close proximity to the hospital.

Shortly before 8 o'clock the prison bell began to toll, and just as the clock was striking the hour a procession was seen coming from the wing of the prison in which Peace had been confined. First came the governor of the prison, Mr Keene, and the under-sheriff, Mr. W. Gray; then came the chaplain, attired in his surplus and reading the service customary on such occasions; and immediately behind was the convict with his arms pinioned to his side and supported by a couple of warders.

Taking his place on the scaffold, the executioner, Marwood, began to bind Peace's legs and adjust the rope around his neck. This done, he was in the act of putting the white cap over his head, when Peace said rather sharply, "Don't I want to look."

Then, as the chaplain came to a certain portion of the service, he said with much fervency, "God have mercy upon me, Christ have mercy upon me."

Thinking he had finished, Marwood again was in the act of putting the cap over his face, when he said, "Don't, stop a bit, if you please."

Then, turning to the four reporters who were standing by, he said in a loud tone, - "You gentlemen reporters, I wish you to notice a few words I am going to say to you. I know that my life has been base and bad. I wish you to ask the world after you have seen my death what man could die as I die if he did not die in fear of the Lord. Tell all my friends that I feel sure they have sincerely forgiven me, and that I am going in to the Kingdom of Heaven at last. Amen. Say that my last wishes and my last respects are to my dear children and to their dear mother. I hope no person will disgrace them by taunting them or jeering at them on my account, but will have mercy upon them. God bless you, my children! My children, each goodbye. Amen. Oh, my Lord God, have mercy upon me!"

Then Marwood placed the cap over his face, and as he was doing it, Peace, in quite a different tone from that in which he had been speaking said. "I should like a drink; have you a drink to give me?"

Taking no notice of the request, the chaplain continued his prayers, but Peace again interrupted, and asked "for a drink!"

The service was now near its close, and just as the chaplain came to the words, "Lord Jesus receive his spirit." Marwood pulled the bolt, and the wretched man disappeared from view. Death was instantaneous."

On March 24th, 1879, Marwood executed James Simms at Newgate for the murder of Lucy Graham a prostitute.

A report from the Old Bailey Archives states:

"A former American seaman who was sentenced to death by Mr Justice Hawkins at the Central Criminal Court on March 5th, for the murder of a prostitute. On the afternoon of Sunday February 9th, 1879, Simms, now a pitman, was drinking with twenty three year old Lucy Graham in the White Hart at Shadwell, in London's east end. Witnesses saw them quarrel over money, and Miss Graham was then overheard asking a William James to join them. James refused and went back to the bar, but as he looked over his shoulder, he saw Simms draw out a razor and run it across Graham's throat. Simms later claimed that he had killed her after she had stolen his wages on a previous meeting; he was executed on March 24th, 1879, at Newgate."

A report from the Times newspaper states:

"Execution at Newgate of James Simm"

"Whilst being pinioned he smiled, and remarked that he was ready. When he reached the scaffold he ran up the stairs and placed himself upon the marks on the drop. Just before the hood was placed he turned smiled again and nodded to the warders. He said he wanted to speak to the governor and the convict said to him "I wish to thank you 'Sir' in particular, and the rest of you officers for the great kindness you have shown me whilst I have been in here." The hood was put on and when the drop fell death was instantaneous."

It was May 12th, 1879, before Marwood had another execution to carry out. The condemned person he had to execute on this occasion was Edwin Smart who was hanged at Gloucester for the murder of Lucy Derrick.

This extract is taken from The Gloucester Journal 1879:

"The murder for which Edwin Smart suffered the utmost penalty of the law on Monday in Gloucester Gaol did not excite very wide interest, but is certainly one of the most remarkable to be found in the annals of crime. The case presents these singular features - a man committed murder with the deliberate purpose of being hanged, never after deviated from his eccentric desire and actually underwent the fatal sentence; the plea of insanity raised on his behalf being disregarded. Such were the facts that their announcement was received with a general conclusion that the man was mad.

At noon on April 2nd, Mr. Charles Cox, commercial traveller of Charfield, asked him, "What's the matter with the poor woman?" When saw the body of a woman lying beside a heap of stones at the side of the road. With a man standing along side her.

The man said, "I have cut her throat."

Mr Cox said, "God bless the woman."

Then came the startling reply from the man. "Oh, I've only murdered this woman".

Mr. Cox drove on in his cart until he met a roadman named Till, whom he sent to watch Smart while he went on to the Police Station. Till found Smart in the same attitude, and the conversation that ensued between them was thus recounted by Till at the trial.

I said to him, "Good morning, Governor is she your wife?" He said, "No, she was a stranger to me."

I said," why didn't you let the poor woman go her way?'

He said, "How far is any Police Station?"

I said, "About a mile."

He said, "I suppose they will soon be here!"

I said, "Very likely."

Then Supt. Critchley came up on his horse and asked, "What have you had happen here?" and Smart again replied, "I have killed the woman."

Naturally, expecting violence, the Superintendent called Till to hold his horse while he secured the murderer, but Till replied, "Oh, I can't do anything," and as the Officer was alighting added, "There's a parcel down there."

"It is the woman's!" Smart was to reply.

On the way to the Police Station Smart was asked, "Do you know the woman?"

"No," he said.

He turned to the Superintendent, 'Don't you?' The Superintendent simply answered 'No'.

The Officer then cautioned the man and said. "You know the charge against you is a very serious one — you must be cautious what you say as it will be my duty to give it in evidence against you at your trial."

The prisoner answered, "All right."

They drove on to Thombury Police Station where he was searched and in his possession were found a coal hammer wrapped in a handkerchief, a razor and two knives all stained with blood. Examination of the body of the woman showed that she had received several blows in the face from a blunt instrument, and her throat had been cut from ear to ear.

The prisoner said he had taken the hammer from his Aunt's house adding, I was tired of my life and did this for devilment. He said he had previously met another woman whom he had resolved to kill but had been deterred by some children coming on the scene. He denied he had any quarrel with the deceased and there was nothing to suggest the commission of robbery or outrage.

It appeared the woman's name was Lucy Derrick and that she was of the lower class and had left her home in Bristol telling her friends she meant to walk to Gloucester to join some man; the identity of such was never established.

The culprit was tried at Worcester before Mr. Justice Hawkins. The Jury, after hearing all the evidence, deliberated in private for an hour and three quarters and returned into Court with a verdict of guilty, appended to which was a recommendation for mercy. The Judge, in passing sentence of death begged the prisoner not to look for mercy but to prepare for his end, and still the prisoner showed no emotion whatsoever.

From the day of his arrival in Gloucester Gaol where the sentence was to be carried out, the man maintained to the last the same frame of mind as had moved him to commit the crime. Mr. Clifton, his Solicitor, had been making zealous efforts since the trial to get the sentence commuted and had forwarded an address to the Home Secretary but to no avail. On the Saturday, Mr. Clifton received a communication that the Right Hon. Gentleman saw no reason to prevent the law taking its course. On the Sunday, the Chaplain administered Holy Communion to the culprit; in the evening, Smart spent some time reading the Bible and ate a good supper before retiring to bed.

Just after seven in the morning, the Under Sheriff entered the cell and claimed the body in the usual legal form. Then to the scaffold and Marwood, the executioner - a rather short, middle-aged man attired in pepper and salt trousers and waistcoat, black jacket and bowler; a noticeable adornment of his attire being a massive Albert chain.

His whiskers and moustache are neatly trimmed, and his hard, shrewd, but not unkindly eyes, quiet, resolute and penetrating. When he has knotted the rope to his satisfaction and taken sundry measurements to ensure for his victim a free drop, he stands patiently surveying the scene. As the hour of eight approaches, Marwood brings forth the leather straps with which he purposes to pinion the culprit and just before eight strikes he enters the condemned cell. And shakes his hand, and says 'come along with me'. Marwood is as adept in pinioning as he is in every other department of his work and without another word he proceeds to secure a strap round the arms and body of the man so as to leave only the wrists free; he gives the necessary signal and the Under Sheriff leads the way to the gallows bearing his white wand of office.

The Chaplain continues reading the burial service, but no sooner is the culprit on the platform than Marwood rapidly pushes forward his work. Another moment and the noose is slipped around his neck, then he draws from his pocket a white cap which he adroitly places over the culprit's face and without the slightest hesitation, and while the Chaplain is reading a prayer, nimbly slips to the back of the gallows where he strikes the handle of a lever and in an instant the platform falls in with a crash and the pinioned form falls, the rope alone remaining visible.

But the long drop has failed to attain its object. Those who have the nerve to look down into the pit see that for four minutes the suspended body swerves and jerks convulsively and the medical gentlemen state that respiration continues during that period. Marwood, evidently chagrined, stands silently gazing at his victim. At last the stillness of death ensues and the body is left to hang for the hour the law demands to ensure the extinction of life.

When the cap is removed from the face the medical gentlemen and Marwood view it. The lividity of the face suggests doubt whether death is due to strangulation or dislocation of the neck, but Marwood emphatically declares the latter effect accomplished but the drop should have been a foot deeper.

When the black flag is hoisted over the prison porch the news is rapidly transmitted through the city and the knowledge that a fellow creature has been put to death is received with awe."

On May 20th, 1879, Marwood was back at Manchester Strangeways Prison for the execution of William Cooper who murdered Ellen Mather.

A report from the Bolton Evening News states:

"Cooper Makes History"

"Forty two year old William Cooper was a former Bolton soldier who was convicted at Manchester Assizes of the murder of Ellen Mather. Cooper and Mather had been courting many years earlier but had split up after a petty quarrel. As a result Cooper had joined the army and left the country, returning just two days after she had married another man. In 1878, Ellen and her husband split up and she began working as a barmaid at the Albert Inn on Derby Street. When Cooper learned of this he became a regular and although she still liked him she had no wish to get involved in a serious relationship. On St Patrick's night, Ellen was asked by her employer if she would like to earn extra money by waiting on a dance at a local hall, so after her shift at the pub she set off on the two mile walk. As she neared a railway station, Cooper tried to prevent her from going to the dance. After a short argument, he cut her throat. Cooper was immediately arrested and charged with her murder. At his trial his defence claimed that he was not guilty of murder but guilty of manslaughter, he committed the crime in an act of passion. The jury was out for seven minutes returning with a guilty verdict. He was sentenced to death and executed in Manchester on May 20th, 1879. This case made history for it was the first execution in Manchester where no press were present to record the scene."

One man from Bolton went to talk to Marwood in Horncastle wanting to know how Cooper had behaved on the gallows. This was his report taken from an article in the Bolton Journal Saturday May 24th, 1879:

"I had met every train from Lincoln for a couple of days but Marwood had not turned up and the evening before I had to return to Lancashire the station master with whom I had formed a friendship called out to me "Marwood's here." Had I been alone I could not have believed that the seemingly feeble old man, who walked with a limp would be him. He was carrying in one hand a black bag, and in the other a parcel and a couple of walking sticks. He called to my companion "Good evening" and passed out of the station, a bystander remarking, with a jerk of his head, "The old beggar has been polishing somebody off."

Mrs Marwood had told me that before he comes home he always goes to his shop, and there I followed him a few minutes later.

His shop is little bigger than a good size cupboard, with one small window. On a glass panel over the door are the words in gilt letters – MARWOOD, CROWN OFFICE.

When I arrived at the place the shutters were up and the door closed. I opened the door and walked in, saluting him with – "Good evening, Mr Marwood." Raising his head from the pile of letters he was perusing – a score at least – he returned the greeting, eyeing me curiously.

As he raised himself up from the seat to an upright position I was surprised to notice his muscular, compact frame. He is a man of about five feet eight inches and quite nimble for his years. He was attired in a dark suit, cutaway coat, and a black choker, white front ornamented with gilt studs. He wore a massive Albert, (watch) with a heavy ring on his left hand, he looked every inch a well to do tradesman. There was nothing in his face to indicate any animal feelings. He is of very dark complexion, and sports a small moustache and whiskers, slightly tinged with grey, and a cleanly shaved chin. His dark eyes, shifting and restless, are wide apart and crested with a pair of beetle brows. His forehead is very expansive, and his almost toothless mouth very firmly cut. He would doubtless be a hard customer to deal with and knows how to drive a hard bargain.

"Now, sir," he says, turning to me, "what would you like?"

"A pair of boot laces" I asked.

He takes out of a drawer a pair, and says, "here are your bootlaces, would you like a couple of cards?"

I replied in the affirmative, and he handed them to me.

I turned the drift of the conversation as to why I was in Horncastle, the execution of the Bolton man who was executed at Manchester.

"Yes, sir, Cooper was his name," suddenly adding, as if I had sprung a mine of suspicion in his breast, "and who are you, now?"

"Oh! I come from Bolton. I was at his trial. I've known his employers for a good many years."

"What was he, what did he do?" He asked.

"He was a foreman brass moulder – a good workman,"

"Was he, indeed?"

"How did Cooper meet his end?" I enquired.

"He died like a man, sir; as brave as a lion, and never flinched. He stood up as straight as a dart, and held out his hand, which I grasped heartily."

I asked him, "Did he say anything when you entered the cell?"

"He did". He said: "You've come to do your duty?" and I answered, "I have sir!"

"I'm ready for you to perform it!" he replied.

"Was he quiet while you strapped him?"

"Very quiet and very cool."

"You don't always find that is the case, I suppose?"

"I do not, sir. They're all not as ready as he was."

"How did he walk to the gallows?"

"As firm as a rock, going straight on without any assistance."

"Did he go under the drop himself?"

"Yes, I had no trouble at all with him – none whatsoever. He was a fine fellow. After I had put on the cap, and just before he went down, he said "The Lord have mercy on my poor insulted wife. The Lord have mercy on my poor insulted children!"

"He was saying them when I pulled the lever. He left this world with the word 'children' on his lips. He died at once. He did not move that much. (Making a slight motion with his finger). I gave him a 9ft 10in. drop – 6 in. more than I ever gave anybody before. It just accomplished what I wanted, and was not an inch too much. The spinal cord was severed, and he met his death like a man."

On May 26th, 1879, Marwood was Taunton for the execution of Catherine Churchill who had murdered her husband by battering him to death and throwing him in the fire. A neighbour told police that she heard a cry of "Murder!" one evening in early March 1879, and next day the body of 82-year-old Samuel Churchill was found in his cottage. His head and shoulders had been burned off. Churchill's wife Catherine, aged fifty-five, claimed that it must have been a terrible accident, as he suffered from fits and must have fallen into the fire. However investigators found a bloodstained billhook in the cottage and more bloodstains on Catherine's clothes. She was arrested and charged.

The motive for the murder was the old man's will. His wife thought he had left everything to a daughter from a previous marriage. Catherine was wrong – she was to be the beneficiary. She was hanged on Monday, May 26th, 1879, in Taunton Prison.

From Taunton Marwood travelled to York for the execution on May 27th, 1879, of John Darcy who had murdered a gamekeeper, William Metcalfe. John Darcy was a clock cleaner who was convicted at York Assizes on May 7th, for the murder of William Metcalfe, an old man of eighty-five, a gamekeeper, from Oulton, near Leeds. On March 4th, two women heard a cry of murder coming from a cottage on an estate and saw a man robbing the elderly gamekeeper. Also in the vicinity were a father and son both named Mosely, the younger of whom grabbed the cottage door handle to prevent the man escaping while his father rushed for assistance. Before the police could arrive, Mosley came back to the cottage and Darcy pulled out his gun, threatening that he would kill them both if the door was not released at once. Mosely and his son sensibly complied and Darcy fled, leaving Metcalfe dead on the floor. He had been battered to death.

Metcalfe's niece told police she had seen John Darcy at the cottage earlier, he was arrested in his lodgings at Hunslet, Leeds. He was identified by the witnesses and was charged. Darcy was sentenced to death and executed on May 27th, 1879, in York. Right up to the moment of the execution he declared he was innocent of any crime. Nevertheless the convict never lost his nerve and walked with coolness to the gallows. His last words on the scaffold were "Lord Jesus, receive my soul." The bolt was then drawn and he died without a struggle.

From York Marwood travelled to Liverpool to execute Thomas Johnson who had murdered Eliza Parton. On March 23rd, Thomas Johnson and twenty-one year old Eliza Parton visited a house of ill repute at Liverpool and after spending an hour or so drinking they went upstairs to a room. Soon afterwards Eliza came downstairs with scratches on her face. Moments later

Johnson followed and without a word, stabbed her in the neck and then rushed out. He was arrested soon after and could offer no defence, claiming that he had done it "through cruelty." The determined-looking and powerfully built man broke down as the sentence of death was passed and he had to be carried in tears by the warders from the dock. He was hanged in Liverpool on May 28th, 1879.

On July 28th, Marwood was at Wandsworth for the execution of Kate Webster for the murder of her employer, Julia Thomas.

This is another one of Marwood's notable cases.

Kate was a rather incompetent career criminal who had served several prison terms for various thefts and offences of dishonesty, both in her native Ireland and in England. These included a period of 12 months in 1877, in London's Wandsworth prison, where she would ultimately die.

A report from the Times Newspaper states:

"She was born Catherine Lawler in 1849, in Killane, Co. Wexford in what is now the Irish Republic and started her criminal career at an early age. She claimed to have married a sea captain called Webster by whom, according to her, she had had four children. Whether this is true is doubtful, however. She moved to Liverpool stealing money for the ferry fare and continued stealing once she arrived there. This was to earn her a four-year prison sentence at the age of eighteen. On release, Kate went to London and took work as a cleaner - often "cleaning out" her employer's possessions before moving on. In 1873, she settled at Rose Gardens in London's Hammersmith area. Her next-door neighbours were Henry and Ann Porter with whom she got on well. They were to feature later in her story. Kate moved to Notting Hill to a new job as a cook/housekeeper to a Captain Woolbest, whilst in his employ, she met a man named Strong with whom she went to live and becoming pregnant. She gave birth to a son on April 19th, 1874, and was promptly abandoned by Mr. Strong. Without any means of support, Kate resorted to her usual dishonest practices and served several prison sentences as a result. On release from Wandsworth in 1877, she again sought domestic work, firstly with the Mitchell family in Teddington, of whom she was to say that they didn't have anything worth stealing.

She was constantly on the move at this time and used several aliases including Webster and Lawler. Sarah Crease, another domestic servant, became friends with Kate somewhere around this period, and it was Sarah who found herself, looking after Kate's son during his mother's spells in prison.

On January 13th, 1879, Kate entered the service of Mrs Julia Martha Thomas at No. 2 Vine Cottages, Park Road, Richmond. To begin with the two women got on well and Kate recorded that she felt she could be happy working for Mrs. Thomas, who was comfortably off. She was a rather eccentric woman in her mid 50's. Soon however, the poor quality of Kate's work and her frequent visits to local pubs began to irritate Mrs. Thomas. After various reprimands, she gave Kate notice of dismissal, to take effect on Friday, February 28th. This period of notice was a fatal mistake on the part of Mrs.

Thomas as she became increasingly frightened of her employee during this time, so much so that she asked friends from her church and also relatives to stay in the house with her. On Friday 28th, as Kate had not managed to find a new job or any accommodation, she pleaded with Mrs. Thomas to be allowed to remain in her house over the weekend. Sadly, Mrs. Thomas agreed to this - a decision that was to cost both women their lives. On Sunday morning (March 2nd, 1879,) Mrs. Thomas went to church as usual. Kate was allowed Sunday afternoons off work but had to be back in time for Mrs. Thomas to go to the evening service. This Sunday afternoon Kate went to visit her son, who was, as usual in the care of Sarah Crease. She then went to a pub on the way back to Vine Cottages. Thus she got back late which inconvenienced Mrs. Thomas, who again reprimanded her before rushing off so as not be late for the service. Fellow members of the congregation noticed that Mrs Thomas seemed agitated; possibly because she suspected Kate's dishonesty and feared her home was being robbed. Whatever the reason, Mrs. Thomas left church before the end of the service and went home, sadly without asking anyone to accompany her. Precisely what happened next is unclear. In her confession prior to her execution, Kate described the events as follows: "We had an argument which ripened into a quarrel, and in the height of my anger and rage I threw her from the top of the stairs to the ground floor. She had a heavy fall. I felt that she was seriously injured and I became agitated at what had happened, lost all control of myself and to prevent her screaming or getting me into trouble, I caught her by the throat and, in the struggle, choked her."

At her trial, the prosecution painted a rather different picture. Mrs. Thomas' next-door neighbour, Mrs. Ives, heard the noise of the fall followed by silence and at the time thought no more of it. Little was she to suspect what was to happen next. Kate, of course, had the problem of what to do with the body but instead of just leaving it and escaping, she decided to dismember it and then dispose of the parts in the river. She set about this grim task with a will, firstly cutting off the dead woman's head with a razor and meat saw and then hacking off her limbs. She par-boiled the limbs and torso in a copper on the stove and burned Mrs. Thomas' organs and intestines. Even Kate was revolted, and sick at the enormous amount of blood everywhere. But she stuck to the job and systematically burnt or boiled all of the body parts and then packed the remains into a wooden box, except for the head and one foot for which she could not find room. It has been said that Kate even tried to sell the fatty remains from boiling the body as dripping. Mrs. Ives was later to report a strange smell from next door (which was caused by the burning). Kate disposed of the spare foot on a manure heap but was left with the problem of the head, which she decided to place into a black bag. She continued to clean up the cottage on the Monday and Tuesday and then, "borrowing" one of Mrs. Thomas' silk dresses, went to visit the Porter family on the Tuesday afternoon, taking the black bag containing the head with her. She told the Porters that she had benefited under the will of an aunt who had left her a house in Richmond which she wanted to dispose of, together with its contents, as she had decided to return to Ireland. She asked Henry Porter if he knew a property broker (estate agent) who might be able to assist her.

Later in the evening Kate excused herself and went off, ostensibly to visit another friend. She returned later without the black bag, which was never found. Both Henry Porter and his son Robert had carried the bag for Kate at various stages of their walk to the railway station and two pubs along the way and both noticed how heavy it was. This left Kate with the rest of the human remains in the box to dispose of and she sought the services of young Robert Porter to help her in this, taking the lad back home with her for the purpose. She and Robert carried the box between them to Richmond Bridge, where Kate said she was meeting someone who was taking the box. She told Robert to go on without her. Robert was to hear a splash of something heavy hitting the water below a few moments before Kate caught up with him again.

The box was discovered the next morning by a coalman. He reported his discovery to Inspector Harber at Barnes police station and the police had the various body parts examined by a local doctor who declared that they were from a human female. He noticed that the skin showed signs of having been boiled. Without the head, however, it was not possible to identify the body.

Kate, meanwhile, was calling herself Mrs. Thomas and wearing the dead woman's clothes and jewellery. She kept up pressure on Henry Porter to help her dispose of the property and he introduced her to a Mr. John Church, who was a publican and general dealer and who she persuaded to buy the contents of the house. Kate and Church seemed to rapidly become friends and went drinking together several times. The real Mrs. Thomas had not been reported missing at this stage and the papers referred to the human remains in the box as "The Barnes Mystery," a fact known to Kate, as she was able to read, as could the Porter family.

Robert told his father about the box which he had helped Kate to carry and which was like the one described in the papers.

Kate agreed a price for the furniture and for some of Mrs. Thomas' clothes with John Church and he arranged for their removal. Unsurprisingly, this was to arouse the suspicion of Mrs. Ives next door, who questioned Kate about what was going on. Mrs. Church was later to find a purse and diary belonging to Mrs. Thomas in one of the dresses. There was also a letter from a Mr. Menhennick to whom Henry Porter and John Church paid a visit. Menhennick knew the real Mrs. Thomas and it became clear from the discussion that it could well be her body in the box. The three men, together with Menhennick's solicitor, went to the Richmond police station and reported their suspicions. The next day a search was made of No. 2 Vine Cottages and an axe, razor and some charred bones were recovered, together with the missing handle from the box found in the river. Thus on the March 23rd, a full description of Kate Webster was circulated by the police in connectio0n with the murder of Mrs. Thomas and the theft of her effects. Kate had decided to flee to Ireland taking her son with her - which was to be the first place the police searched for her. She was arrested on March 28th, and kept in custody awaiting collection by two detectives from Scotland Yard. She was brought back to England and taken to Richmond police station where she made a statement on March 30th, and was formally charged with the murder. The statement accused John Church of being responsible for Mrs. Thomas' death and he was subsequently arrested and charged with the murder, too. Fortunately, he had a strong alibi and had also assisted the police in discovering the crimes. At the committal hearing, the charges against him were dropped while Kate was remanded in custody. She was transferred to Newgate Prison to save the long journey by horse drawn prison van across London each day for her trial.

Her trial opened on July 2nd, 1879, before Mr. Justice Denman at the Central Criminal Court (the Old Bailey) next door to Newgate. In view of the seriousness of the crime, the Crown, was led by the Solicitor General, Sir Hardinge Gifford, and Kate was defended by Mr. Warner Sleigh. A hat maker named Mary Durden gave evidence for the prosecution telling the court that on February 25th, Kate had told her she was going to Birmingham to take control of the property, jewellery, etc. that had been left her by a recently deceased aunt. This, the prosecution claimed, was clear evidence of premeditation, as the conversation had occurred six days before the murder. One of the problems of the prosecution case, however, was proving that the human remains the police had found were actually those of Mrs. Thomas. It was a weakness that her defence sought to capitalise on, especially as without the head there was no means of positively identifying them at that time. Medical evidence was given to show that all the body parts had belonged to the same person and that they were from a woman in her fifty's. The defence tried to suggest that Mrs. Thomas could have died of natural causes, in view of her agitated state when she was last seen leaving church on the Sunday afternoon. Both Henry Porter and John Church gave evidence against Kate describing the events in which they had been involved, and her defence again tried to point the finger of suspicion at them. In his summing up, the judge, however, pointed to the actions and previously known good characters of both of them. Two of Kate's friends, Sarah Crease and Lucy Loder, gave evidence of her good nature. Late on the afternoon of Tuesday, July 8th, the jury retired to consider their verdict, returning just over an hour later to pronounce her guilty. Before she was sentenced, Kate yet again made a complete denial of the charge but cleared Church and Porter of any involvement in the crime. As was normal, she was asked if she had anything to say before she was sentenced and claimed to be pregnant. She was examined by some of the women present in the court and this claim was dismissed as just another of her lies. She went back to Newgate and was transferred the next day to Wandsworth to await execution. It has been suggested that Wandsworth did not have a condemned cell at this time although it would seem unlikely. In any event, Kate was guarded round the clock by teams of female prison officers.

Kate was to make two further "confessions" in Wandsworth the first implicating Strong, who was the father of her child. These allegations were also found to be baseless.

Kate was informed by her solicitor that no reprieve was to be granted to her, despite a small amount of public agitation for commutation. So on the eve of her hanging, Kate made another confession to the solicitor in the presence of the Catholic priest attending her, Father

McEnrey, which seemed somewhat nearer the truth. She stated that she was resigned to her fate and that she would almost rather be executed than return to a life of misery and deception.

The execution was, as usual, to take place three clear Sundays after sentence and was set for the morning of Tuesday, July 29th, at Wandsworth prison.

Kate was to be only the second person and the sole woman to be hanged there.

At 8.45am, the prison bell started to toll and a few minutes before 9.00am the Under Sheriff, the prison governor, Captain Colville, the prison doctor, two male warders and Marwood formed up outside her cell. Inside, Kate was being ministered to by Father McEnrey and attended by two female wardresses. She would have typically been offered a stiff tot of brandy before the execution commenced. The governor entered her cell and told her that it was time and she was led out between the two male warders, accompanied by Father McEnrey, across the yard to the purpose built execution shed. Having the gallows in a separate building spared the other prisoners from the sound of the trap falling, and made it easier too for the staff to deal with the execution and removal of the body afterwards. As Kate entered the shed, she would have been able to see the large white painted gallows with the rope dangling in front of her, with its simple noose lying on the trapdoors. Marwood stopped her on the chalk mark on the double trapdoors and placed a leather body belt round her waist to which he secured her wrists. Then he strapped her ankles with a leather strap. She was not pinioned in her cell, as became the normal practice later. She was supported on the trap by the two warders standing on planks set across it. This had been the normal practice for some years in case the prisoner fainted or struggled at the last moment. Marwood placed the white hood over her head and adjusted the noose, leaving the free rope running down her back. Her last words were, "Lord, have mercy upon me." He quickly stepped to the side and pulled the lever, Kate plummeting down some eight feet into the brick lined pit below.

Kate's body was left to hang for the usual hour before being taken down and prepared for burial. The whole process would have taken around two minutes in those days and was considered vastly more humane than Calcraft's executions. The black flag was hoisted on the flagpole above the main gate, where a small crowd of people had gathered for her execution. They would have seen and heard nothing and yet these rather pointless gatherings continued outside prisons during executions until abolition. As the criminal was female no newspaper reporters were been allowed to attend the execution but the Illustrated Police News did one of their famous drawings of the scene as they imagined it, with Marwood putting the hood over a pinioned Kate's head. Later in the day, her body was buried in an unmarked grave in one of the exercise yards at Wandsworth."

On August 8th, 1879, Marwood wrote a letter to the Governor, H M Prison Cork, Ireland.

Sir,

"Pleas this is to inform you that i reseaved your kind letter Consering a Prisoner now under Sentence of

Death at H M Prison Cork Ireland i sent you a Telegraph Message staiting that i would send you a letter this Day to arainge for the Time. Sir Pleas this is to inform you that Monday and Tuesday the 25 and 26 Days of the month Sugest is ingaged in England if you will be so kind as to arainge your Time I wi come over to cork and Execute the Prisoner Sir I hope it will not make any Diffeance to you in Regard to the time Pleas I should be very glad if you would be so kind to arainge to appoint Friday the 22 or 29 day of August for the Time for the Execution to take place at Cork – pleas if you will arainge for the time you may Depend on me to arrive at the Time appointed and i will Bring all things that is wanted for the Execution Rope and straps and cap Pleas Set one back your Reply as i Shall Return Home on Tuesday next from Exeter the 12 Day of August I shall be very glad to hear From you in the Matter in forthwaith Sir I Remain your Humble Servant Wm Marwood"

On August 20th, 1879, Marwood wrote another letter to the Governor of H M Prison Cork.

"Sir, Pleas I feel viry sorrey that ham not able to attend at Cork on Monday to Execute the Prisoner as ham ingaged tow Execute tow prisoners in London on that day and Tusday to Execute a prisoner at Warwick then will com Direct to Cork Ireland. Pleas to get the Sheriff now that he as the Power to arainge the Time for my coming over thear wil not aney Truble acor in arainging the Time i Thank the Sheriff for is kindness but cannot Execute the Prisoner on Monday the 25 day but will on Friday the 29 day

Pleas let me have a letter by the return of post

Remaim Your Humble Servant Wm Marwood"

Since there are no records of Marwood going to Ireland on that date we can only presume that the authorities got someone else to commit the execution.

On August 11th, 1879, Marwood executed another female, Annie Tooke, at Bodmin for the murder of six-month-old Reginald Hyde. Reginald was born on October 6th, 1878, to a young woman called Mary Hoskins who had moved to Exeter to conceal the pregnancy. She was persuaded to give up the child by her brother to nurse Annie Tooke. Annie could not cope with the growing baby and murdered the child by suffocation. She cut up the body and hid some of it in the coalbunker. When Annie was arrested, she described how the child had been taken away from her a fortnight earlier, then changed her story saying how she cut him up with a firewood chopper on the coal bunker. Mr Edward Stookes, found the torso of the child in the leat (open watercourse) of Powhay Mill. The body parts were taken to the Alexandra Inn to be examined by a surgeon. Annie Tooke was tried at Exeter on July 21st, and 22nd, 1879, and executed on August 11th.

On August 25th, 1879, Marwood executed James Dilley at Newgate for the murder of the bastard child of Mary Rainbow by giving it laudanum, hitting its head with a blunt object, then throwing it over a wall where a builder, doing a job on the wall, found it. A police investigation was made and Dilley was charged with the murder and executed. The day after, Marwood was in Warwick for the execution of John Ralph who had murdered Sarah Vernon.

The last execution of the year was carried out at Ipswich on December 3rd, 1879. The person who Marwood executed was Henry Bedingfield who murdered Eliza Rodden. Bedingfield, a stonemason, was often heard saying, "I'll kill any man who tries to borrow Eliza's pony and cart. In fact, I'll kill any man who even looks at her." This was all a bit presumptuous of him, since he was a married man, and Eliza, who lived near him in Woodbridge Road, Ipswich, was only his mistress.

By May 1879, Eliza herself was beginning to get worried about his jealous attention. She told him: "You shan't borrow my pony and cart yourself, neither!" Bedingfield became very angry. Yelling and shouting abuse, he stormed off. Next day he went back to Eliza's home, cut her throat, and then botched an attempt to cut his own throat.

"He attacked me!" Eliza gasped at horrified witnesses who arrived in time to watch her die, while her lover lay groaning on the floor. At Norwich Assizes four months later Bedingfield claimed: "She went for me before she took her own life." The jury decided that it didn't happen like that, and gave a guilty verdict. He was hanged on Wednesday, December 3rd, 1879, in Ipswich Prison, still claiming he was innocent.

Chapter Nine – Executions 1880

The first execution of 1880 was carried out at Newgate on January 5th. Marwood's culprit was Charles Surety who had murdered a child aged two. Twenty nine year old Surety was a bricklayer who was sentenced to death by Mr Justice Lindlay at the Central Criminal Court, for the murder of the daughter of his girlfriend, thirty-two-year-old Mary Ann Pepper. Evidence showed that Surety had brutally ill-treated the unfortunate child. On one occasion he bashed it against a door. He also expressed a wish to lay the child on the floor and thrash her till she couldn't move; and to starve her. The actual cause of death was probably a beating with the fists. His execution caused a controversy when, as Marwood completed his preparations and Surety had only a matter of minutes to live, an express letter arrived at the gaol carrying a reprieve. The Governor, after a conference with other officials, decided that the letter was a forgery and the execution went ahead as planned. It was later discovered that a London doctor who received a prison sentence and heavy fine for attempting to obstruct the course of justice wrote the letter, for no apparent reason.

On January 16th, Marwood was in Galway, Ireland for the execution of Martin McHugo who murdered Michael Breheney. McHugo was convicted at his third trial after the first two ended with the jury failing to agree on a verdict, of the murder of Michael Breheney. He had become incensed at Breheney who was taking out proceedings against him for defamation of character. On Christmas Eve, 1879, McHugo followed Breheney down a quiet country lane at Woodford, County Galway, and battered him to death with a large stone. He pleaded an alibi but the presence of a piece of cloth in the dead man's hand which matched perfectly with a piece torn from McHugo's raincoat was enough to convince the jury of his guilt.

On February 17th, after a month at home, Marwood was back in Manchester Strangeways Prison for the execution of William Cassidy who murdered his wife. Cassidy and his wife had been married for many unhappy years and after a series of rows, he decided to be rid of her. He told a friend in a pub that he intended to kill his wife and he would swing for her. One night in November 1879, Cassidy crept into her room as she slept and after soaking the bed in paraffin he set it alight. His wife awoke engulfed in flames and rushed down the stairs into the arms of a policeman who had called to the house to investigate a flash of light he had seen in the bedroom. She was taken to hospital in agony and later died from her burns.

At his trial Cassidy claimed his wife had been drunk and whilst smoking in bed must have fallen asleep and knocked the paraffin lamp over onto herself. But the prosecution proved otherwise and he was sentenced to death. Cassidy was executed on February 17th, 1880.

On March 2nd, Marwood was back again at Liverpool's Kirkdale House of Correction for the double execution of Patrick Kearns and Hugh Burns who murdered Patrick Tracey at Widnes, on October 24th, 1879

The history of the crime and the execution is taken from the Liverpool Daily Post March 3rd, 1880:

"Double execution at Kirkdale yesterday."

"Both Patrick Kearns and Hugh Burns, labourers, were executed yesterday morning, at about a quarter past eight o'clock, at Kirkdale Gaol, for the murder of Patrick Traccy at Widnes, on the 24th, October last. The prisoners were condemned at the late Liverpool Assizes, together with Mary Anne Tracey, the wife of the murdered man. The female culprit being enceinte, the judge, Lord Chief Justice Coleridge, ordered a respite in her case.

For the first time in Liverpool since the passing of the law which made executions private, the representations of the press were excluded from witnessing the scaffold scene, the prevention being apparently due to the action of the High Sheriff, Mr William Garnett, of Lancaster. The governor of the prison also gave instructions to the officials tantamount to decline all information to the Press, insomuch as in answer to an application to see the governor after the execution, the warder at the gate gave the 'general reply to the reporters that the governor had directed him to say that the inquest would be held at ten o'clock.'

The circumstances of the executions yesterday made the exclusion of the Press probably more unsatisfactory than might have been anticipated, as there was not only a report circulated by a friend of Kearns that the culprit had declared his fellow-prisoner, Burns, guiltless of the murder and, that he would make a confession to that effect, but even in the executions themselves a very unusual delay of a quarter of an hour took place. At the inquest which followed upon the executions, the governor of the gaol said that he had no knowledge of any confession whatever made by Kearns, and as to the delay in carrying out the sentences, he explained that was due to the fact that both the Sheriff and the Under Sheriff had first gone to Walton Gaol by mistake, and that afterwards suffered the mishap of a breakdown of the vehicle – a wheel came off – in which they were travelling.

Shortly after seven o'clock, Marwood, who was the executioner, and who had remained on the previous night at the Court House public house, Kirkdale, was admitted to the gaol. About ten minutes past eight, the High Sheriff, who had hurried up on foot, was admitted to the prison; and soon afterwards the Under Sheriff, who likewise walked, gained entrance to the building.

Notwithstanding the extreme inclemency of the morning, the ground being covered with melting sleet and snow, while snow continued to fall briskly in the thickest of flakes, there was a crowd in the neighbourhood of the gaol numbering about sixty persons. These consisted mainly of working men from the immediate locality and a few women and children of the lowest class, as might be judged from their attire and general appearance. It was said that some of the labouring classes present had come from Widnes, where the murderers were known, but this could be only verified as far as two men were concerned. One of these was a young man who had been a friend of Kearns, and another said he was a second cousin of Kearns's, and had travelled especially from Ireland to see him, but was refused admission, as he had come too late. This young man not only lamented the stringency of the rules which excluded him from seeing his condemned relative, but also spoke strongly of the exclusion of the reporters from the execution. He likewise said that it was a great injustice to hang Burns. Burns who was a native of Carlow, seemed to have no relatives present. Neither of the two culprits were married, it was said.

Considerable uncertainty prevailed amongst the crowd as to the exact moment of the execution. At eight o'clock the black flag was run up upon the tower, but it was immediately taken down again, and many thought that the execution had taken place, and accordingly left the vicinity of the gaol wall where they were listening for the thud of the falling men. The prison bell, however, continued to toll from a little before eight until a quarter past when the flag was finally displayed to the public view.

Except for the presence of the crowd, as has been stated, the only other indication outside the walls of

Kirkdale Gaol that anything unusual was taking place inside was furnished by the fact that a few cabs, which had brought fares to the prison, were drawn up outside, as was also a small detachment of borough police under the superintendence of an inspector, who yesterday discharged duties of this kind for the twenty second time, and with the courtesy and kindness of demeanour of which friends and relatives of unhappy culprits must have had from time to time some grateful experience.

It came out at the inquest that the drop given to Kearns was eight foot seven inches and Burns was given nine feet six inches being the lighter of the two culprits. Mr James Barr, surgeon of the gaol said – I was present at the execution this morning, which took place in due form. There were no irregularities whatsoever or anything to complain of. I have seen the deceased from time to time, and saw them both yesterday. Technically, the cause of death was dislocation of the vertebrae. The spinal cord was severed in each instance. Death would have been instantaneous. There was no struggling. I saw the two culprits bodies taken down and removed to the pressroom. I there satisfied myself that death was complete.

THE HISTORY OF THE CRIME

….."As far as Patrick Kearns and Hugh Burns were concerned the motive for their crime was little more than the comparatively small and vulgar one of robbery. In the case of Kearns it is true that there may have been said also a motive of jealousy, he having been upon improper terms of intimacy with the murdered mans wife, who was herself an accomplice to the assassination. She duly awaits the birth of her child before she also undergoes the extreme penalty of the law for her complicity in the foul deed. In such a depraved person as Kearns was, however, the motive of jealousy may be almost left out of the consideration, as to such a coarse nature as his the motive of simple greed was likely to operate not only with greater but with all-absorbing force. In the case of the condemned woman, the motive of illicit love may have swayed her more largely, as the evidence showed not only the extent of her improper intimacy with Kearns, but the systematic manner in which she had endeavoured to secure what, to her would be a large sum of money upon her husbands death presumably for the purpose of facilitating her union with her paramour after her husbands death.

Insurance upon the murdered mans life was developed at the insistence of the wife to an extent not only out of all proportion to the deceased position and means, but too plainly for the purpose of serving the object Mrs Tracey must have had in contemplating his murder. Tracey's life was insured to no less an amount of £364 11s. and as far as £350 of the sum at least, Mrs Tracey knew of the existence of the polices, of which it appeared also from the evidence that Kearns also was probably aware. The murder was committed in the early morning by a shot from a pistol while the deceased lay in bed in his house on the 24th. In October 1878, an insurance policy for the sum of £100 was effected on the life of the deceased in the Prudential Insurance Company, and a few months prior to that an insurance for £250 had been effected in the Accident Company. In the month of March 1879, some conversation took place between an agent for the Prudential Company and the deceased man and wife, the two latter being then apparently under the impression that in the case of Tracey's death the sums payable under the policy would be immediately paid. The agent told them that such would not be the case, but if they effected a small insurance it would be paid immediately on death. Accordingly a new policy was taken out for the sum of £14.1s. was effected on the life of Tracey, which came into force just a fortnight before the murder. For some time before the murder Mrs Tracey had began speaking to the agent of the Wesleyan and General Insurance Company with the view of insuring her husbands life in the further sum of £100. The agent ascertaining that the mans life was already insured in the large sums mentioned, declined to take an insurance on his life, and expressed his great surprise that one in the position of Tracey should have been insured to the extent he was. As far as the insurance upon the man's life – the realisation of which would seem to have been the main motive of the murder – were concerned matters rested in his position at the time of the murder.

Of the improper intimacy between Mrs Tracey and Kearns, the evidence at the trial left no substantial doubt. Kearns lodged in the deceased's house, as did Burns, but only for a short time before the murder. On the morning of the murder the neighbours who lived at either side of Tracey's house were roused by noises in his house. One of the neighbours went into the house immediately, and saw the deceased lying dead in bed in a room up stairs, he having been evidently killed by a shot, which had made a large wound in the head. A statement was made by Mrs

Tracey, and was adopted by the two lodgers who were present, to the effect that a burglary and robbery had been committed, and that a box in the lower part of the house contained £15 had been broken open and rifled, and that the burglars had afterwards come upstairs and had shot Tracey as he lay in bed with his wife and infant child.

Mrs Tracey said "that the sound of the shot awakened her, and that she at once got up and knocked at the doors of the lodgers and aroused them."

This statement was to prove to be false by the evidence particularly of Dr. O'Keefe, who was summoned to the scene of the murder, and by a Mrs Fahey, one of the neighbours.

Dr. O'Keefe said "that while there was no mark of blood either upon the clothing of Mrs Tracey or that of the child, a large streak of blood, which must have spurted from the deceased head, lay along the bed, and must have marked the clothing of anyone who might have laid there."

Mrs Fahey also stated that "whereas she was awakened by a noise of the shot she heard no sound of knocking at a door or cries of alarm afterwards such as had been described by Mrs Tracey."

The appearance of things inside the house was also inconsistent with the story of the burglary. The dust and cobwebs near the window through which it was suggested robbers had effected an entrance remained undisturbed, as were also a number of little things upon a table which lay in the way of anyone coming into the house in such a way as was suggested. Evidence at the trial likewise showed that both Kearns and Burns were concerned before the murder in the purchase of a pistol such as that with which the deed had apparently been committed. The male culprits were immediately apprehended and the female shortly afterwards, consequent upon evidence which transpired, principally as to the undisturbed condition of the dust on the window, and the absence of any blood stains upon her night clothing.

Kearns whilst in Kirkdale Gaol, wrote a letter to Inspector Thomas Barnett, of Widnes, soliciting an interview with him relative to the murder. In the interview which followed a few days afterwards, Kearns made a long statement, incriminating the culprit Burns and exculpating himself. In some time after his condemnation, which tool place at the last Liverpool Assizes, before Lord Chief Justice Coleridge, on the second day of the trial of the three culprits, Kearns, it was stated, withdrew his confession, and declared it to be false, Burns having had no share in the crime.

The jury, after twenty minutes deliberation, found the three prisoners guilty and Lord Chief Justice Coleridge, in passing sentence of death upon them, expressed his full concurrence in the verdict. The female prisoner being advanced in pregnancy, the judge respited judgement in her case, leaving the date of her execution unfixed for the time being."

On going through the records of females executed, there is no record of a Mrs Tracey ever being executed for her part in the crime. Burns, right up to the time of the execution, protested his innocence. He seemed to have had no one to take sufficient interest in him to get up a public petition for his reprieve, beyond the statement of Kearns exculpating Burns, which has already been stated.

On March 22nd, Marwood executed John Wingfield at Newgate for the murder his wife. Wingfield was tried at the Old Bailey on March 1st, 1880. After ill-treating his wife she left him taking their children with her. Wingfield had permission to take them at weekends then he found out that she was going to a dance hall with one of his workmates and letting his children starve. Wingfield got a knife and stabbed his wife in front of witnesses, who were too horrified or too frightened to intervene. He inflicted no fewer than seventeen wounds upon her. He was arrested sent for trial and sentenced to death. The children were put into care.

The Times carried the report of the execution the next day:

"John Wingfield who was tried before the Justice Grove was executed yesterday for the wilful murder of his wife at Newgate where he had been confined since his condemnation. His defence stated that Wingfield was insane but the jury convicted him. Since his trial the prisoner has behaved in an exemplary manner. He took farewell of his children and other relatives on the Friday last. And the sentence was carried out yesterday. Death was instantaneous, and he was buried within the prison grounds."

On April 14th, Marwood was back in Omagh, Ireland, for the execution of Peter Conway who murdered James Miller. Mr Justice Harrison sentenced Conway to death for the murder of James Miller, his brother-in-law, at Pomeroy in July 1879. The Conway family were struggling to pay for the upkeep of their smallholding and had to mortgage the land to pay the bills. Through abject poverty, Peter Conway killed Miller on July 14th, and then robbed him of some money. Witnesses saw Miller call at the Conways after he had spent the day fishing; he was never seen alive again. When his body was found battered to death a few miles away the next day, Conway and his father were arrested. Conway senior was acquitted at the trial but his son was later executed in Omagh on April 14th, 1880.

Marwood carried out Aylesbury Prison's last execution on May 10th, 1880. The condemned person he executed was William Dumbleton who murdered John Edmunds.

This report was taken from the Aylesbury Journal:

"They called him Gentleman Johnny. He had given up the penury of farm labouring to make his own way as an itinerant clock and watch repairer, walking from village to village near his home on the Buckinghamshire/Oxfordshire border.

He earned a good living at it too, enough to be considered prosperous.

And now here he was at 10 o'clock in the morning lying dead in a ditch at the roadside, with his head almost cut from his body.

The man who discovered the body at Piddington was a travelling draper from Berkhamsted named Thomas

Plenderleith. He went for help and when the police arrived he ventured an opinion: "He looks like he's been run down by a horse and cart, don't you think?"

Inspector George Webb shook his head. To him it looked more like murder. He wanted to find out where and with whom Gentleman Johnny – real name John Edmunds, 35 – had spent the previous evening.

The locals were full of information. Johnny was at the Seven Stars at Ludgershall all evening. They remembered him showing the other customers a couple of watches he'd bought – one of them worth more than 20 times the price he'd probably paid for it. The landlord gave the inspector the names of four labourers who were drinking at the bar with Gentleman Johnny.

Inspector Webb called on the first, William Dumbleton, who shared a bedroom in a two-room cottage with his brother, two sisters and their mother. He began to lie outrageously when questioned, and when police searched his home they found Gentleman Johnny's expensive watch hidden in the thatched roof of an outhouse. Then Dumbleton began to tell a different story.

He said he was with another man he named as James Sharpe. "He borrowed my knife. I stayed behind a hedge while he knocked Johnny down, and then I went up to them. When I got there he'd cut Johnny's throat. After we had given him enough, we chucked him in the ditch and left him. I was very drunk that night."

Later, in another statement, he said he cut the victim's throat himself.

Dumbleton was brought to trial at Northamptonshire Assizes on April 20th, 1880. And convicted and despite the jury's recommendation for mercy on the grounds that he had a defective upbringing, James Sharpe wasn't arrested for lack of any other evidence. Found guilty of murder, Dumbleton went quietly to his death on the gallows on Monday, May 10th, 1880, in what was the last execution at Aylesbury Prison."

One day later, May 11th, 1880, Marwood was in York Castle for the execution of John Henry Wood who murdered John Coe.

The York Library local Archives supplied this item:

"They met in a pub in Whiston, near Rotherham, and after a few drinks they began a serious pub-crawl. In the small hours of February 18th, 1880, they ended up in a brothel near Rotherham town centre. Their names were John Wood, a labourer and a recently released burglar, John Coe, both aged twenty-seven years old. No one can be quite certain what happened after they left the brothel, but next morning Coe's body was found in Canklow Road. His head had been battered in by a heavy branch which a passer-by had seen Wood carrying. Wood was arrested in the act of attempting to steal Coe's watch, and was convicted of the murder at York Assizes in April 1880. He was hanged on Tuesday, May 11th, 1880, at York Prison."

On July 27th, 1880, Marwood was in Maidstone for the execution of Thomas Berry who murdered Carolyn Adams.

On August 3rd, 1880, Marwood wrote a letter to B. Scott Currey, Under Sheriff, Derby as follows:

"Sir Pleas This is to inform you that i have Reseaved your Letter this Day Conserning the Prioner now under the Sentence of Death in H-M-Prison Deby the Time you have appointed for the execution to take place is Monday the 16 Day of August 1880 at 8 oClock Sir This is To inform you that i will ingage with you to Execute the Prisoner at the Time you have apointed and i will ariave at the Prison on Saturday the 14 Day of August you may Depend on me to ariave at the time you apointed and i will bring Rope and Straps when i Com Sir you Wanted now My Fee thear is Won Fee that is for the unieted Kingdom is the saim as Reseaved at Derby at the Last Execution that is £10-0s-0d for the Execution with Travlin Expenisis Thear is no Charge for Time nor for Rope and straps thea found by me are from the Home Office London in my Charge in Cair

Sir I Remain your Humble Servant Wm Marwood Church Lane Horncastle Lincolnshire"

On August 16th, 1880, Marwood was in Derby for the execution of John Wakefield for the murder of Eliza Wilkinson, a little comb-box seller aged nine years old.

This extract is taken from The Derby Evening Gazette, Monday August 16th, 1880:

"At his trial at the Assizes on July 29th, the tale of his crime ' The murder of the little comb-box seller' is not likely to be soon forgotten.

In Bridge Street in this town there were sojourning for a time a man named Wilkinson and his family who were maintained by the manufacture of boxes made of paper and conveniently constructed so to hang in a convenient place near where the dressing or ablution is performed in humble domiciles, and large enough to contain combs and other small toilet requirements. The man who was the maker of the boxes, employed two of his daughters to retail them at halfpenny each wherever the little saleswomen could find customers. On the morning of April 26th, in pursuance of their humble calling, they found their way into Green Street when the elder of the two sisters saw Eliza the younger who was only nine years of age, pass into an entry towards what is known as Tan-yard, and that was the last time she or any one else but her murderer would seem to have seen her alive. That she was decoyed into the house where Wakefield was alone, and was afterwards found there cruelly, brutally, and ruthlessly butchered, and that the man gave himself up as the self-accused assassin, are the only facts that are definitely known. What transpired in that house no human eye observed, and no human ear heard? The murderer and his victim were alone in the deadly struggle; and even sought refuge from himself and from the scene of his crime within the clutches of the officers of the law. The man would appear to have given himself up at once to the police, a self-proclaimed murderer, and so collected was his manner that the experienced officer believed him to be one of those men 'fond of fallacy,' who have a fancy for associating themselves with some atrocious crime or criminal. But the visit of the chief constable to the miserable house told the fatal truth and the dead corpse of the comb seller was found lying in a pool of blood. The dreadful penalty of an ignominious death by the scaffold was this morning paid to the unhappy culprit, John Wakefield, who has been made to experience the full rigour of the righteous law which sweeps the murderer from the land of the living. The revolting records of ensanguined deeds which incarnadine the criminal annals of the country, contain very few instances of a crime apparently as devoid of motive or meaning as that of which Wakefield was convicted. Revenge, jealousy, hatred, and plunder – all the incentives that prompt and lead on desperate and brutalised minds to acts of deadly violence, are conspicuously absent from the narrative of the crime; and have thus left it to stand out in disgusting prominence for its cold-blooded and wanton disregard of the sacredness of human life. The culprit has consequently been left to his fate without a shade of that charitable sympathy which is sometimes galvanised in to action even for the most desperate and degraded of villains; which took the form of a memorial to the Secretary of State for the Home Department, with whom it rests to advise Her Majesty in the exercise of her prerogative of mercy; but neither the high official referred to nor the reverend judge who tried the case – and whose emotion when pronouncing the awful sentence of the law was an index in him of goodness of heart – could see no reason for arresting the complete execution of the sentence, for which Marwood, the executioner, arrived in Derby on the Saturday."

The Official report of the execution states:

"John Wakefield was hanged within the precincts of Derby Gaol this morning. The scaffold was erected on the usual site at the north front of the building, and at about half past seven o'clock Marwood, the executioner, was engaged upon his final arrangements The convict retired to rest on Sunday evening at the usual time, and slept until one o'clock this morning, at which hour he was awakened by an attack of toothache, which ailment had troubled him considerably of late. In fact, he was unable to court sleep successfully afterwards. He arose soon after five o'clock and dressed himself. At about seven o'clock he was served with a light breakfast, although he had indicated his indisposition to partake of any refreshment whatever. He remained in his cell until a few minutes before the clock struck eight, when the Under-Sheriff, accompanied by the Sheriffs officer, presented himself and demanded "the body of John Wakefield for execution." A procession was formed, headed by several warders, and including the Governors of the prison, the chaplain and the police surgeon and the convict himself, who walked quietly but firmly between the warders. It was barely five minutes to eight when the little company reached the spot assigned for the purpose of pinioning. Here they were met by Marwood, who assisted by two of the warders, effectively secured their prisoner in the usual way. The procession was re-formed, and made for the scaffold, which, by the way, was situated only a few yards distant. The convict still preserved his composure. He did not even turn pale when the scaffold came in to view, and mounted the steps with an unfaltering gait. While the rope was being adjusted, the prisoner prayed fervently, but in a very low voice, so quietly indeed that his utterances were audible only to those by whom he was immediately surrounded. His last words are stated to have been "Lord, receive my spirit." The chaplain, meanwhile, was repeating fragments of the Church Burial Service, and at the very moment he repeated the words "Man that is born of a woman hath but a short time to live, the bolt was drawn and the prisoner literally fell a lifeless corpse. Death was to all appearances, instantaneous. The "drop" allowed the prisoner who, though stouter than when he was apprehended, is yet a man of lightweight, was nine feet six inches in length. The body was taken down at nine o'clock and an inquest was held at three o'clock in the afternoon."

Outside the gaol:

"At half past seven o'clock there had gathered a knot of about a couple of hundred persons in the precincts of the gaol, and these gradually increased until the whole area immediately fronting the building was crowded. There were at least 3000 persons present. The only gratification of their desire for the sensational was a full view of the prison walls, the dismal sound of the passing bell, and the occasional presence on the parapet of a warder, who had to make preparations for hoisting the black flag, the signal to the world outside that the work of the hangman was completed. The crowd for the most part consisted of boys and girls, though there were not a few well-dressed men and women. The cages on the high telegraph posts, which to some extent overlooked the gaol, were fully occupied, and a very large number of persons had located themselves on the Great Northern viaduct, from which a view of the gaol buildings was commanded. Meanwhile amongst the crowd was recognised a brother of the condemned man, and he immediately became an object of considerable curiosity. He assumed an air of perfect indifference, and even whistled as if to show an absence of undue excitement – a manifestation of fraternal feeling, which did not gain approbation from the spectators. He took refuge in a beer-house adjacent, where he added boasting and bombast to his affected callousness. This, it seems, was the only brother the prisoner expressed any desire to see. As the clock struck eight up went the dark flag, a subdued groan rose from the assembled throng and most of them then quietly dispersed. A small body of police was present to preserve order, but no great demand was made on their services. The drawing of the bolt and the swinging of the stage could be distinctly heard from outside."

The following notice was posted outside the prison door:

"Declaration Of Sheriff and Others."

"We, the undersigned, hereby declare that judgement of death was this day executed on John Wakefield, in Her Majesty's Prison in Derby, in our presence. Dated this 16th day of August 1880. B. Scott Currey, Under Sheriff of the County of Derby. C. E. Farquharson, Governor of Her Majesty's Prison at Derby. Henry Moore, Chaplain W. Barclay Delacombe, Officer to the Sheriff of Derbyshire. Walter J. Piper, Public Journalist.

Certificate of Surgeon:

I, John Wright Baker, the Surgeon of Her Majesty's Prison, at Derby, herby certify that this day examined the body of John Wakefield, on whom judgment of death was this day executed in Her Majesty's Prison at Derby, and that on examination I found that the said John

Wakefield was dead. Dated this 16th, day of August 1880."

After having some time at home with his wife, Marwood's next execution was on November 16th, 1880, when he executed William Brownless for the murder of his sweetheart, Elizabeth Holmes, at Evenwood, near Bishop Auckland, on August 18th.

On November 20th, 1880, Marwood was in St. Albans for the execution of Thomas Wheeler who murdered Edward Anstee.

A report from the St. Albans Journal states:

"The three early-morning visitors at Marshall's Wick Farm, Sandridge, just outside St. Albans, struck terror into the owners. As the farmer, Edward Anstee, 58, opened an upstairs window to see who was calling, he recognised the trio – all members of the notorious Wheeler family. Mr. Anstee didn't have long to reflect on what to do. One of the men, Thomas Wheeler, 46, raised his shotgun and blasted the farmer to death. The terrified housekeeper locked herself in her bedroom as the three marauders ransacked the farm for anything of value they could find.

When they had gone and the police investigated, the Wheeler family were obvious suspects. But only Thomas Wheeler stood trial at Chelmsford Assizes in November 1880, and he was hanged on Monday, November 29th, 1880, at St. Albans Prison."

Curiousley, ten years later, James Berry executed Wheeler's daughter, Mary Eleanor Pearcey, for another murder. Berry described her as "the most beautiful woman he had ever hung, with her big blue eyes, and masses of wavy hair. She had lips like Cupid's bow." Berry was spellbound when he saw Eleanor in her cell. He confessed that he did not like to execute her but the law said Eleanor should die and she did on December 23rd. Berry gave her a drop of six feet, six inches longer than Marwood had given her father.

On November 22nd, 1880, Marwood was at Bristol for the execution of William Joseph Distin who murdered Elizabeth Daniels. On August 27th, Elizabeth, a widow who lived with Distin as his wife, stormed into the local public house and made him come home for his dinner. A friend of Distin's joined them and they sat down for supper apparently on good terms. Soon after the friend left, Mrs Daniels, bleeding from a wound to the shoulder, staggered into their landlady's room, where she collapsed and died. Distin was recommended for mercy at the trial on the grounds that the crime wasn't premeditated. The Judge thought otherwise and Distin was hanged.

On November 22nd Marwood received a letter from the governor of Newgate prison enquiring if he would be prepared to carry out the executions of George Pavey and William Herbert on the usual terms. He replied saying he would and on December 13th, Marwood was back at Newgate for the executions of William Herbert who murdered Jane Messenger and George Pavey who murdered Ada Shepherd, aged ten.

A report from the Times Newspaper, 1880, states:

"Twenty nine year old George Pavey was sentenced to death by Mr Justice Hawkins at the Old Bailey for the murder of Ada Shepherd who was a young girl of ten. The young girl's father had left her alone in the house with Pavey while he went out. When he returned he found the child dead in the kitchen with her throat cut. She had also been violently raped.

At his trial the father of the child gave evidence.

"My name is John Shepherd. I am a house decorator, of Herbert Villa, Cooper Road, Acton—the prisoner worked for me—on 22nd, October my family consisted of myself, my wife, my daughter Ada, and four other children, the youngest was a baby—Ada was 10 years of age; she would have been 11 on 10th, December next—on 22nd, October I and my wife went out at 11.30, taking the baby with us, and leaving the other children at home—before we left I asked the prisoner to have an eye to the place, to wait with the children till we came home, and to light the gas—he said he would do so—I am not certain whether we went out by the front door; we generally go out the back way—the side door was open—we returned about 6.30 at night—there was no light in the house—we went in at the front door; I let myself in by a latch key—I proceeded to the kitchen, and called for the prisoner and for the children—I got no answer—I then went to the kitchen door; I found it locked—the key was on the outside—I turned the key, and opened the door—when I got into the kitchen I found my child Ada lying on her back before the fireplace dead, with a handkerchief over her face—I went over the way to Mr. Lessingham's, a friend of mine, and got some matches, and came back and lit the gas—I then found my child lying perfectly straight, with the handkerchief over her face; the legs were towards the door, straight out; her arms by her side, and her throat cut—the police were sent for—nothing was moved out of its place till the police came—I found that the side door was fastened on the inside with a bolt, and the back door the same—I went over the house directly I had lighted the gas—I found the door of the back bedroom on the first floor forced; I had left it locked, and my wife had taken the key—there was a box there unlocked, and there was a till inside the box; the till had been forced by a screwdriver of mine and a sum of money and Pavey was missing."

Pavey was arrested in a Hendon workhouse wearing bloodstained clothing. At trial his plea of not guilty was unsuccessful and he was executed alongside William Herbert in Newgate on December 13th, 1880.

William Herbert's trial took place at the Old Bailey on November 23rd, 1880. Jane Messenger's husband gave evidence. "I am Henry James Messenger. I live at 41, Edward Square, Islington, and am a wood turner. The prisoner is the husband of my late wife's eldest sister. His home was at Footscray, in Australia, he arrived in this country on 16th, March and he stayed at my house from 18th, March to the 16th, August, five months all but three days. On 16th, August the prisoner, my wife, and her brother left my house, not together, but within a quarter of an hour of one another; my wife had not my permission to go. I saw her again on 8th, October but I did not know where she was living between 16th, August and 8th, October. On 8th, October she came to the place where I worked, 69, Southampton Street, Pentonville. On the 11th, I saw the prisoner; he came to my work in the morning. I told him if he waited till dinner-time I would fetch his letters, and give them to him. I did so, and he gave me an acknowledgment. I asked him if he had seen my wife; he said he could take his Bible oath that he had seen nothing of her since 16th August, when they left my place, since that time I have had no conversation with him. On 21st, October my wife returned to my home; she only slept there on that night. On Friday morning, the 22nd, I went to my work and when I returned home at dinner-time; my wife was not there. She did not sleep at home on the night of the 22nd."

Another witness gave evidence.

"My name is Sarah De Boo, I am a widow and live at 45, Stonefish Street, Notting Hill, on 8th, August a friend of mine brought the prisoner and Mrs. Messenger, and her brother to my house; they wanted two rooms. I had but one to let, they came again on 16th, August, together, about 3 o'clock in the day, and were given the room they continued to live at my house for seven or eight weeks. They had one common room, and Mrs. Messenger slept in my parlour. She had a child with her, and the child slept with her, they took their meals together in the common room, there was a bed in that room. The prisoner and his brother Sam slept in that bed. In the day time they were all together upstairs. Sam went out sometimes. The prisoner and the deceased were sometimes left alone in the upstairs room. I can't say exactly how long Sam stayed there; it might have been four or five weeks, and then left. After he left the prisoner and the deceased continued to occupy the upstairs room during the day time, she continuing to sleep downstairs with the child as before; the child was between three and four years of age. I used my parlour in the day time, and I used to sleep there as well as the deceased and her child when the other rooms were occupied.

In the morning the deceased used to go upstairs to the room where the prisoner was, when she had dressed herself. The prisoner left my house a week before Mrs. Messenger; he left on the Saturday morning as she left on the Thursday evening following, 21st, October. She told me she had taken a room for him somewhere else.

I never saw her again alive after she left on the Thursday evening, when I last saw them together they appeared to be on good terms, I never saw them any other way but on good terms."

A witness to the shooting then gave evidence.

"My name is John Bradley, I live at 25, Chatterton Street, Finsbury Park. I am agent to a railway company, on Friday, 22nd, October, about 12.30 in the day, I was entering Finsbury Park from the Blackstock Road and I saw the prisoner there with a lady; they were entering by the same gate walking side by side. They took the path to the north of the inner circle of the park—I lost sight of them for a short time—I saw them again about 10 to 15 minutes later — they were then sitting on one of the seats opposite the lake—they were in conversation. I then made my way out of the park, as it had commenced raining and as I was going along, I heard a report of a pistol, that was about four or five minutes after I had seen the prisoner and the lady sitting on the seat. I at once turned round and saw the lady running away from the prisoner towards me; he was running after her trying to catch hold of her. I ran towards them, and saw the prisoner fire at her breast. I saw the revolver; he had hold of the woman's shawl with his left hand and fired with his right. She fell on her knees, held her hands up, and appeared to implore the prisoner to spare her, and looked at him in the face. He fired at her again, he aimed at her breast; I was not more than three feet from her when he fired that shot, she then fell forward on her face. He then threw his overcoat on one side with his left hand and put the revolver to his breast with his right hand and pulled the trigger and fired, he reeled for a short distance and fell on his side—two or three gentlemen came up—the prisoner got up again with the revolver in his hand and walked in front of the deceased and the gun fell out of his hand— I called for a policeman and he was taken away to the hospital."

A doctor at the hospital gave evidence.

"My name is Frederick James Gant. I am a Fellow of the Royal College of Surgeons. I saw a good deal of the prisoner in the hospital; he was my patient there, apart from the wound he appeared to be suffering from very great depression. He several times alluded to the attempt on his life. On the second or third day after his admission he said that he was tired of his life; that it was no use my showing him the attention. I did, to endeavour to restore him, he was tired of his life that was the state of his mind during all the time he was there."

Jane Messenger's husband gave more evidence.

"On the 23rd I went to the Great Northern Hospital, between 10 and 11 in the morning; I there saw the dead body of my wife".

The jury gave a guilty verdict and George Pavey was executed on December 13th, 1880, alongside William Herbert.

By this time Marwood was not exactly contented with the old-fashioned English method of 'happy despatch' by hanging, and sought to acquire fresh ideas upon the subject by consulting foreign models. For this purpose Marwood sent his nephew, who was supposedly destined to become his successor, to study the noble art in foreign lands.

In the Life and Career of Marwood The Executioner, Purkless wrote:

"Professor Marwood, as the young man is designated in America, where he has chosen to study the first rudiments of the profession to which he hopes to succeed, is a promising young man, adopted and educated by Marwood himself, who has no sons of his own. Young Marwood is the produce of the present epoch – a child of our time – a reasoner, a student, a hunter of waterfalls. He has been taught to consider effect and cause as dependent on each other, and so bent upon visiting the condemned convicts before the execution, as well as pending and after. Needless to say that young Marwood is meeting with every facility in the United States, where hanging is considered one of the lightest of professions – an occupation without risk of soil or blemish to the person. It appears that he does not treat the science of hanging lightly, but takes it as much au serieux and as deserving investigation as any other; and after visiting the principle gaols, he has set about examining, with a critical judgment, the different methods of treatment of the criminals, both before the execution and at the very moment of it taking place, and has given especial attention to their necks. After much deep study he comes to the flattering conclusion that the English mode of capital punishment is decidedly the best and most humane."

Glasgow's old Gallows used until 1868

Full size reproduction of the Nottingham gallows
Nottingham's Galleries of Justice, 2009
Marwood carried out four executions in Nottingham.

One of William Calcraft's old ropes.

The type of executioner's rope used right up to the last execution in 1964.

Front and reverse of one of William Marwood's cards.

The Execution of Thomas Gray

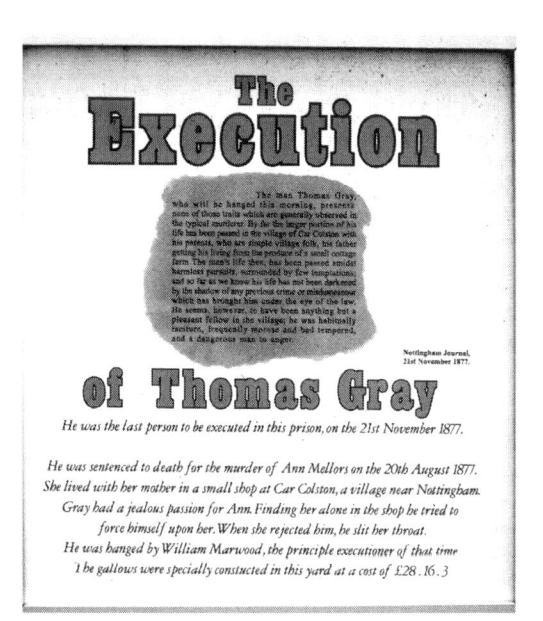

> The man Thomas Gray, who will be hanged this morning, presents none of those traits which are generally observed in the typical murderer. By far the larger portion of his life has been passed in the village of Car Colston with his parents, who are simple village folk, his father getting his living from the produce of a small cottage farm. The man's life then, has been passed amidst harmless pursuits, surrounded by few temptations; and so far as we know his life has not been darkened by the shadow of any previous crime or misdemeanour which has brought him under the eye of the law. He seems, however, to have been anything but a pleasant fellow in the village; he was habitually taciturn, frequently morose and bad tempered, and a dangerous man to anger.
>
> Nottingham Journal, 21st November 1877.

He was the last person to be executed in this prison, on the 21st November 1877.

He was sentenced to death for the murder of Ann Mellors on the 20th August 1877.
She lived with her mother in a small shop at Car Colston, a village near Nottingham.
Gray had a jealous passion for Ann. Finding her alone in the shop he tried to
force himself upon her. When she rejected him, he slit her throat.
He was hanged by William Marwood, the principle executioner of that time
The gallows were specially constucted in this yard at a cost of £28.16.3

Notice on the wall.
Nottingham's Galleries of Justice, 2009.

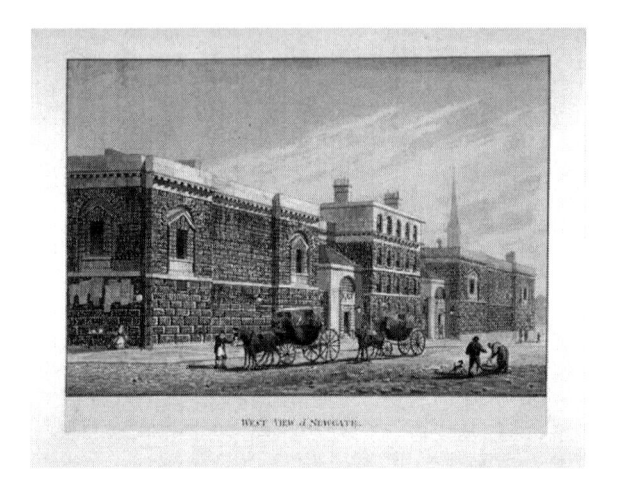

Print of Newgate Prison by George Shepperd
Marwood carried out seventeen executions at this prison.

> Horncastle
> Sep 26-1881
>
> Mr. W. Roe
> Derby
>
> Dear Sir,
> in Answer to your Letter This is to inform you that the Late Charles Peace was Executed at H.M. Prison Armley on Tuesday the 25th Day of February 1879 the Execution took Place at Armley Prison near Leeds Yorkshire
>
> Wm Marwood
> Executioner
> Horncastle

Copy of the letter written by William Marwood to Mr. W. Roe, dated 26 September 1881.

William Marwood the man himself.

The first written article on Marwood appeared in 1890.

Entrance to Kilmainham Gaol, Dublin Where Marwood executed 'The Invincibles' 1883,
I, the copyright holder of this work, hereby publish it under the following license:

This work is licensed under the Creative Commons Attribution-ShareAlike 3.0 License.

James Burton, Marwood's last execution August 6th, at Durham 1883.
Durham Prison.

Spilsbury Road Church and Churchyard, where
Marwood and both of his wives are buried.
All the graves in the churchyard are now unmarked.

Marwood's first appointment at Durham was a triple hanging on the 5th of January 1874 other hangings were carried out here by Marwood, including two triple executions, one double and his last one James Burton.

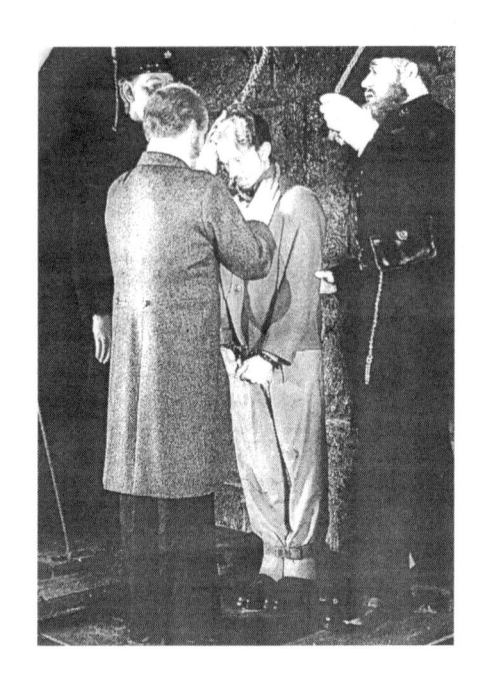

A Madame Tussaud's Exhibition

Chapter Ten – Executions 1881

The first execution of 1881 took place at Chester on February 21st, when Marwood executed William Stanway for the murder of Ann Mellor. Stanway, a native of Newcastle-under-Lyme, earned a living as a broom maker and hawker. He was convicted at Chester Assizes of the murder of Ann Mellor at Macclesfield, where they lived with their nine-year-old daughter. Both Stanway and Mellor were addicted to drink and frequently quarrelled, which usually ended with Stanway giving Ann a beating. Shortly after Christmas 1880, they went out drinking one afternoon and later, when they returned home, he beat Ann up. Stanway went out again that evening, leaving Ann in bed; when he returned he called for Ann to come and fix him some supper. Ann at first refused to come down but William eventually persuaded her. When Ann reached the foot of the stairs he stabbed her in the chest with a red-hot poker. Stanway didn't call a doctor for two days, during which time Ann lay in extreme agony and by the time help arrived, she had died. At Stanway's trial, his defence stated that the crime was not premeditated, the jury rejected this statement and he was executed on February 21st, 1881, in Chester.

Marwood's next execution was at Derby on February 28th, 1881, when he executed Albert Robinson for the murder of Elizabeth Bagnall.

Marwood's next execution was on May 17th, 1881, at Maidstone. Albert Moore, a soldier, murdered Mary Ann Marsh, a seventy-four year old woman. On February 15th, Mary was left in charge of 'The Woodlands,' the residence of a Lieutenant Scriven of the 52nd Regiment, at Gravesend, during his temporary absence. On his return Lieutenant Scriven found Mary dead inside the house. Her throat had been cut from ear to ear. Moore, a private in the Regiment, who worked as the Lieutenant's batman, was identified as the man seen leaving the house shortly before the murder was discovered. He was arrested, charged with the murder and executed. On the scaffolding Moore showed no sign of remorse for the crime he had committed.

Marwood's next execution was James Hall, executed at Leeds Armley on May 23rd, 1881, for murdering his wife. This Sheffield cutler killed his licentious wife, Polly, by splitting her head in two with an axe. Shortly before midnight on March 26th, Hall's daughter and her boyfriend walked home from a pub and found they were unable to gain entry into the house. Looking through the window, the daughter saw her father standing over her mother holding a hatchet. After repeatedly knocking on the window, Hall eventually opened the door and as the young couple entered, Hall struck his daughter in the face with the weapon. Her boyfriend managed to overpower Hall, while a neighbour, who had been attracted by the commotion, called the police.

Once in custody, Hall confessed to the murder and explained his motive. He claimed that three years earlier he had come home from work unexpectedly to find his wife with another man. He later forgave her but warned that if she was ever unfaithful again he would kill her. At 11pm on the night of the crime, Hall came home from the pub sooner than usual and found his wife on the sofa with a neighbour, William Londe. Mrs Hall grappled with her husband while Londe made his escape. Then, in a violent, drunken rage, Hall picked up a hatchet and attacked her. His daughter denied that her mother was an adulteress, as did Londe, who claimed he was nowhere near the house on the night in question. Hall was sentenced to death at Leeds Assizes and hanged.

On the May 31st, 1881, Marwood was in Liverpool where he executed Joseph Patrick McKentire for murdering his wife. McKentire was a Liverpool born tailor who had been married to his wife Ellen for twenty-four years. They had spent the last two decades living unhappily. On April 4th, he got very drunk in a local public house. His wife was later found lying in a pool of blood on the bedroom floor. She had been beaten to death with a broom handle. McKentire was arrested on April 7th, trying to find lodgings in nearby Garston. He was tried at the Liverpool Assizes, found guilty and was executed on May 31st, 1881.

Marwood was in Nottingham on August 15th, 1881, for the execution of Thomas Brown who murdered Eliza Caldwell.

This article comes from The Nottingham Journal 1881:

" Shocking murder this morning in Nottingham"

"About two o'clock this morning a shocking murder was committed in Batley Street, Arkwright Street, Nottingham. It appears that for some time past a man by the name of Brown has been living with a young woman named Caldwell, and it is said they kept a questionable house in the above street. For some reason or other they had a serious quarrel, which ended in Brown cutting the woman's throat in a most shocking manner, from ear to ear, the head being nearly severed from the body, of course life being quite extinct when the police entered the house.

Brown was immediately apprehended and taken to the London Road Police Station and from there to St. John Street. Most likely the prisoner will be brought before the magistrates this morning, and charged with the murder. His trial took place at the Midsummer Assizes found guilty and sentenced to death by Mr Justice Steven."

On Monday 15th, August Thomas Brown was executed.

The following report was supplied by Nottingham Local History Library and is reproduced with the permission of the newspaper:

"As early as seven o'clock a small number of persons assembled at the corner of Glasshouse Street and the adjacent places to the gaol, and every arrival at the gaol entrance was watched with anxiety. No public announcement having being made as to the failure to procure a reprieve, there was perhaps some uncertainty as to whether the sentence would be carried out; but when the daily papers had spread the news, the populace flocked to the vicinity of the gaol in large numbers, and at eight o'clock there were several thousand present who seemed eagerly discussing the proceedings inside.

At a quarter to eight o'clock the bell of the gaol rang out in slow, deliberate and solemn tones, and at ten minutes to eight, Marwood joined the party assembled, carrying in his hand strong leather straps for the pinioning of the unfortunate convict.

Marwood seemed rather flushed and nervous, made grave respectful salutations to those assembled, and when handed the Sheriff's warrant for the execution he received it with a low bow and a formal expression of thanks. In reply to one or to questions the executioner said the arrangements at the scaffold were very good; he also explained how he had arranged the scaffold and further stated that he had several sets of straps for pinioning, and that the set he carried with him were last used in Liverpool. He was very respectably dressed and wore a ring with a large stone in it on his little finger. He said he had only seen the prisoner in the distance.

At six minutes to eight one of the prison warders announced that the time had arrived for fetching the convict from the cell to the scaffold, and the gentlemen assembled then proceeded down the wide open corridor to the B wing of the gaol. The convict was in cell number 10, and into this cell Marwood entered with the turnkeys. The prisoners was pinioned in the course of a couple of minutes and brought into the corridor and the procession was formed to the scaffold in the following order:

The Sheriff, the Under Sheriff, his Bailiff, the Governor, the Chaplain, the Surgeon and the convict being between two warders followed by Marwood and three reporters from the local newspapers and a further three warders. As the procession moved towards the scaffold the Chaplain read aloud in a distinct tone the words, "I am the resurrection and the life" from the Church of England burial service. The pinioning interfered with the prisoner walking but he seemed perfectly calm, his eyes were steady and he showed no sign of fear on his face. He wore a dark coloured coat and a waistcoat, grey trousers and a pair of shoes which were, rather worse for wear, in the button hole of his coat he wore a large red camellia, highly inappropriate to the occasion.

When the scaffold was reached the officials and others arranged themselves in half a circle around the structure. When Brown took his stand on the drop he still maintained firmness. No exclamation escaped from his lips and he never flinched when the executioner placed the white cap on his head and adjusted the rope. As the Chaplain was uttering the words which tell us that all is vanity, the bolt was drawn and the drop fell with a heavy thud, and Brown was in eternity. The drop given was nine feet four inches and death must have occurred instantaneous, judging from appearances. The unfortunate innocent flower lay at the bottom of the hole. Immediately after the execution the black flag was hoisted on the turret of the gaol.

The inquest was carried out at four o'clock in the afternoon and he was buried a short time later within the grounds of the prison."

On August 5th, 1881, Marwood received a letter from the governor of Newgate prison informing him that the date for the execution of William Nash would be the August 22nd, and inquired if he would he be available to carry it out. Marwood had to decline the offer, as he was due in Maidstone the following day for the execution of George Durling who murdered Fanny Mussen.

Thirty six year old George Durling was convicted at the Old Bailey on August 5th, of the murder of Fanny Mussen, aka Frances Vincent aged twenty-five, with whom he lived in lodgings at Woolwich. Both were heavy drinkers and as a result they had frequent drunken quarrels. On July 20th, they had a fight in the street, during which Durling threw bricks at Fanny and threatened to kill her before the night had ended. They made up and walked home together, but on reaching the garden adjacent to their lodgings, the quarrel started up again. This time Durling picked up an iron carpet-beater, swung it around and smashed it into Fanny's head with such force that it penetrated her skull to a depth of four inches. She died at once. Realising what he had done, Durling fell to his knees and began kissing her and begging her forgiveness. He was arrested and immediately confessed his crime. He was executed in Maidstone Prison on August 23 rd, 1881.

On November 21st, Marwood had another execution to perform. For this he had to travel to Derby. The person he had to execute on this occasion was Alfred Gough who murdered six-year old Eleanor Windle.

On August 20th, a group of young children were picking blackberries in a field at Brimington, near Chesterfield. At around 9.30am Gough, a hawker, passed by the group with his barrow and soon after one of the children, six-year-old Eleanor, told her friends that she was going to follow him and ask for a toy from his barrow. Gough was later seen with the young girl in Johnson's Lane and quite soon after, she was found dead. She had been raped and strangled. Gough was arrested on suspicion of murder after he told a friend that he knew something about the crime. Later, witnesses testified that they had seen a bundle on his barrow around the time the girl vanished. Gough was convicted at Leicester Assizes on November 2nd, and confessed in the condemned cell to the Governor. He was executed on November 24th, 1881, and later buried in the prison grounds.

Marwood was in Manchester Strangeways Prison on November 28th, 1881, for the execution of John Aspinall Simpson who murdered his girlfriend, Ann Ratcliffe. Twenty -three year old Simpson was an unemployed clerk from Preston and had been courting sixteen-year-old Ann Ratcliffe for over eighteen months although her parents didn't approve of the relationship. Later, when she became pregnant, her father, a Preston publican, forbade Simpson to see his daughter again and then changed his mind and told Simpson he had to marry her. Early in the morning of August 3rd, which was the day of the wedding, Simpson called to see Ann at the pub. While her father was upstairs, Simpson cut her throat with a cutthroat razor, which he had stolen from a barber's shop. Simpson was quickly arrested and tried at the Manchester Assizes. One of his ex-girlfriends told the court he had no intention of marrying Ann. His defence claimed that Simpson had told Ann on the morning of her death that the wedding could not go ahead and so she took her own life. He was convicted and sentenced to death. The sentence was carried out in Manchester on November 28th, 1881.

Marwood's last execution of the year took place at Lewes near Brighton and Hove. The person he executed was Percy Lefroy Mapleton who murdered Isaac Gold. This was another of Marwood's notable executions.

Lefroy had set out one morning in June 1881, to rob any poor unfortunate who crossed his path. Failing to find a victim at London Bridge station, he ended up on the 2pm train to Brighton where he came across a wealthy merchant named Gold. Lefroy shot and stabbed Gold to death and stole his watch and a few gold coins. Lefroy was spotted getting off the train at Preston Park where he claimed to have been the victim of a robbery himself. Despite obvious signs of his involvement, he was allowed to escape and remained at large for ten days. After he was caught, he was tried at Maidstone assizes and found guilty of murder.

This account of Lefroy's execution appeared in the Daily Telegraph, November 30th, 1881:

"Lefroy saw his executioner as he entered the cell. Then it was probably too late for much thought. "I hope the rope will not break," was the only expression to which he gave utterance, possibly the result of some apprehension from what he had heard of the "Marwood long drop".

There was not time for more, the hangman was already busily at work, passing the leather belt round his body, fastening his elbows and wrists, and baring his neck. The bell was tolling, and nine o'clock had nearly come. It was time to be moving. The clergyman, in his white surplice, was ready; two warders had taken their places, one on either side of the condemned; Marwood, with one strap yet unused in his left hand, and his right hand firmly fixed on the leather belt that confined his victim, was prepared to move; the under sheriff, the governor of the jail, surgeon, and magistrate all were waiting; it was time for the burial service to begin. The corridor echoed forthwith to the sound of the death prayer. Slowly passing through the passage towards the door that led into the yard moved that awful procession; and as the warder unlocked the door, which opened, close by the scaffold it emerged into the air. I had chanced to see Lefroy on several previous occasions, and notably at the trial, and yet it was with a feeling bordering upon curiosity that I now looked upon him as he emerged into the open. There was much that operated against the producing of a favourable impression: he was attired, not, as had been stated, in a prison garb, but in a very old suit of greyish tweed; he was tightly pinioned, so tightly that, as I afterwards observed, his wrists were bruised; his hat was off, and his hair somewhat disarranged; he had not been shaved for some time; and he was being hurried along by his executioner at a disquieting rate. But apart from all this, there was a pallor on his face so unearthly that he presented the appearance of one who was already dead, and I much doubt whether, but for the presence of the warders on either side of him, and the support which he gained from the hangman who pushed him forward, he would have been able to accomplish the distance from his cell to the grave. The words of the clergyman, rising and falling upon the ears of the spectators, were evidently lost upon him; he did not appear to hear the passing bell, but looked upwards as though in an agony of fear, and so stumbled helplessly along. It was not far, only a few score yards in all, but the march to the grave, or rather to the scaffold, seemed terribly painful; all the bravado that was witnessed in the dock at Maidstone had gone; the terrors of death were in full force upon the hapless culprit. As he approached the scaffold this was particularly noticeable; he could scarcely take the step, which was to place him where he had never stood before and from whence he would never step again, and Marwood, who at no instant left go of the belt, was fain once more to push him forward. It was evidently not the moment for ceremony with the hangman, who was now once more very busy placing the tall young man, up to whose shoulders his own face scarcely reached, under the cross tree, stooping down to strap up his legs, and then fumbling about with a white glazed linen cap which he now assayed to put over the trembling youth's face. I do not suppose for a moment that Marwood intended to be rough; he was possibly excited, and anxious to do everything as expeditiously as possible. But it certainly appeared to me that in attempting to fix the cap on Lefroy's head, and in pulling it down over his face, he hurt the prisoner somewhat unnecessarily. The worst of this was, however, yet to come. The long rope dangling about Lefroy had now to be adjusted, and the thimble through which the noose ran to be placed beneath his neck. I did not time it; it may have lasted only a few seconds; but to me it seemed appallingly long, while the swaying of Lefroy's body showed the agony he was enduring. I cannot tell whether the sound of the clergyman's voice, which continued all the while the preparations went on, was of great consolation to him. His last look as the white cap was produced was lifted heavenward, his pallid face turned upwards, his lips moving as though in prayer; but so soon as the cap was over his face he began to sway, so much that I expected he would fall before the business was finished. At last, however, all was ready, and Marwood, grasping the hand of his victim, stepped back; there was another awkward pause, apparently for the purpose of allowing the clergyman to finish the sacred invocation in which he was engaged; and then the lever being pulled back, the trap doors opened, and Lefroy falls with a terrible thud into the cavern below. Down 10ft, as was presently shown by the measurement of a tape line, he had dropped, the whole weight of his body falling upon the neck, which, receiving such a strain, was instantly broken so completely that the body never gave so much as one convulsive shudder, but, turning half round, hung swaying in the cold morning air, enveloped by a haze of steam rising from the corpse, and showing, by the visible disconnection of the vertebrae and by the open hands, how sudden death had been.

The preliminaries to the hideous spectacle had been painful in the extreme, to spectators and sufferer alike. But I think the actual death was as merciful as it could well be, if the agony of the two or three minutes from the leaving of the condemned cell to the fall of the scaffold be left out of consideration. Had there been an assistant to expedite the movement upon the scaffold, or had chloroform or another benignant anaesthetic been given to the condemned to lessen the pain of suspense, fewer faults might have been found with the miserable business.

As it was, without any feelings other than those of reprobation for the horrible crime for which Lefroy suffered, I felt that the agony of death had been unnecessarily prolonged, and that, compared even with the punishment of the guillotine in France, it was a tedious and horrible form of execution. It may, too, have been fancy; but it seemed that the actual falling of the trap doors and the long drop occupied a sensible period; though it is impossible to say how long the two seconds or so thus occupied may seem to one who is being thus awfully despatched. But the whole of the spectacle connected with the Lefroy execution was not over. An inquest had yet to be held on the body of the dead man, and for this purpose a number of the inhabitants of Lewes had been summoned as jurymen. Thus, a little after 10 o'clock, we found ourselves – spectators of the execution, jail officials, coroner, and jury men – convened in the committee room of the prison once more, for the purpose of determining how Percy

Mapleton Lefroy "now lying" to quote the words of the commission, "dead within the precincts of the jail," had come by his end. The jury, sworn in, now proceeded to view the body, and were conducted to the infirmary of the jail, the same room in which, by the way, Lefroy was incarcerated prior to his trial – a large apartment, containing three or four beds and a bath. Here, on trestles, in a shell coffin, lay the dead body of the man, clad as we saw him when he emerged into the yard where he was executed, with his boots still on, and the same grey tweed suit. He had evidently been measured for his coffin while alive, and placed in it but a minute or two before we arrived.

A more horrible appearance than the remains presented is difficult to conceive. And, as though to add to the horrors of the scene, it appeared to be the duty of the jurymen to examine the body minutely, and by prods and pushes to satisfy their curiosity as to the physique of the dead man. In truth his dead body did present the appearance of more strength than I had supposed, and there remained less cause for wonder in my mind as to how he contrived to kill a well-built man such as Mr Gold.

The viewing over, the jury returned to the rooms, and there sat in solemn conclave, while the governor of the jail gave evidence of the identify of Lefroy, and the surgeon deposed to the effect that the deceased met his death by hanging; and then we filed out into the open air once more and the bright sunlight; the mists had gone from the Sussex hills, there was no cloud in the blue sky, and the day, so unusually ushered in to us, was as gladsome as though it had been the herald of spring."

Chapter Eleven – Executions 1882

The first execution of 1882 took place at Devizes, Wiltshire on January 30th. The man Marwood went to execute was Charles Gerrish, a seventy-year-old man, who murdered Steven Coleman. On Thursday, November 24th, 1881, the two old paupers, Gerrish and Coleman, were sitting in front of a fire in a Devizes workhouse. The two men began to quarrel after Gerrish told Coleman that it was his turn to get warm. When Coleman refused to move, Gerrish withdrew a red-hot poker from between the bars in the grate and thrust it into Coleman's neck. Coleman died instantly. The police were called and Gerrish was charged with Coleman's murder. After being convicted at the Wiltshire Assizes, he was executed on January 31st, 1882.

Madame Tussaud produced a waxwork display in 1883 of this execution, using the original suit of clothes that Marwood wore.

Marwood returned to Manchester Strangeways Prison for his next execution on February 13th. The person he executed was Richard Templeton who murdered his landlady, Betty Scott. In May 1881 Richard Templeton took lodgings with Mrs Betty Scott who ran a boarding house at Lowerhouses, Burnley. He was given a room on the first floor, opposite Mrs Scott's room, which she shared with her three children and her brother, who was a cripple.

Within a short time after moving in, Templeton started a relationship with Betty and she often shared his bed. When Templeton lost his job as a printer he took to drinking, often coming home drunk. Betty asked him find other lodgings.

On the morning of January 2nd, 1882, Templeton went out drinking with another of Betty's lodgers and once again came home drunk. At the meal table there was a row over his condition and he went to his room. During the night he got up went to Betty's room and slashed her throat with a razor. After hearing the door close the brother called her several times but got no reply. This awoke the other boarders who went to investigate and found her dead in her bed. The police were called and Templeton was arrested.

At his trial at the Manchester Assizes, his defence tried to prove Templeton was insane but this was dismissed and he was found guilty and told by Justice Chitty that he was to be executed.

On April 27th, 1882, Marwood was at Wandsworth for the execution of George Lamson who murdered his brother-in-law Percy John Malcolm, a cripple suffering from a disease of his spine.

This abridged Times report May 6th, 1882, states:

"It was on December 3rd, last year that Lamson committed the murder for which he on Friday morning answered with his life in Wandsworth Gaol. His victim being his brother-in-law, Percy John Malcolm, a cripple suffering from disease of the spine, the youth in his nineteenth year, and at the date of his murder was a scholar at Blenheim House School, Wimbledon.

On the day mentioned Lamson, in the presence of Mr. Bedrook, the principle of the academy, administered in a capsule sufficient aconitine to produce death. Lamson after the murder left England, but on December 8th, presented himself at Scotland Yard to report his whereabouts and was then taken in to custody and charged with the wilful murder of Percy John Malcolm.

From the Wandsworth Police Court he was committed to the Old Bailey on the capital charge, and, after the trial was found guilty by the jury and sentenced to death. The execution was fixed for April 4th, but representations from the President of the United States that affidavits of importance bearing on the sanity of the condemned man were being sent from America induced the Home Secretary to grant a reprieve to April 19th. Further reasons were urged for a still further respite, and Friday 28th April was fixed for the date of the execution.

Lamson woke on Friday morning last week at an early hour, after having had a tolerably good night's rest. Soon after he rose the chaplain of the gaol entered the condemned cell, and from that moment forward, save during the interval of breakfast, the convict was engaged in devotional services.

On the previous day the scaffold had been got ready, and there was no noise to disturb the culprit as he ate or pursued his devotions. The drop, used on two previous occasions, had already been fitted together, and Marwood had inspected that on the afternoon before, and found that the pit was of insufficient depth and directed that a further eighteen inches should be dug out. This was done without causing any noise.

At about a quarter to nine the bell of the gaol began to toll, greatly disturbing the condemned man, who now learned his time, had nearly come. Very shortly afterwards the Under-Sheriff, the Deputy Governor, the surgeon and four warders made their appearance in his cell, with a view to preparing the convict for his last act. Lamson, who had donned the suit of black which he wore at his trial, was allowed to walk freely from his cell between two warders, at about five minutes to nine, in the direction of the scaffold. That structure chanced happily to be hidden from the point of view of the door by which the culprit emerged by a corner of the wall, so that he could not see it or the grave newly dug at first. Marwood, who was waiting within the inner gates, with his straps thrown over his arm, only hesitated till the cortege should come near him. Marwood, with uplifted hand, had called out 'Halt!' and the procession had stopped. That word 'halt' told its tale upon the prisoner. Realising to the full his position for the first time, to all seeming, Lamson now staggered and almost fell against one of the warders who supported him. His tremor was, indeed terribly apparent, and it was a great question for a moment whether he would fall. The executioner at this instant came to his aid, and with the help of the warders kept him in an upright position.

Not removing the collar which Lamson had put on, and only turning in the points, which might presently stand in the way of the rope, Marwood began to pinion him. "I hope you will not hurt me," the convict murmured, half in fear and half by way, possibly, of remonstrance.

"I'll do my best not to hurt you; I'll be as gentle as I can," responded Marwood, and the work went on.

Marwood's plan here was apparent, Lamson was a more powerfully built man than he appeared, weighing upwards of eleven stone twelve pounds, and the executioner, evidently thinking his strength would operate somewhat against a sharp and quick fall, fastened back his shoulders in a manner which precluded all possibility resisting the action of the drop.

At last the gallows was reached, and here the clergyman bade farewell to the prisoner, whilst Marwood began his preparations with the rope and the beam overhead. With a view to meet any secretions of fear might now befall the culprit, a wise provision had been made. The drop was so arranged as to part in the middle, after the fashion of two folding doors; but lest the doomed man might not be able to stand upon the scaffold without assistance, two planks of deal had been placed over the drop, one each side of the rope, so that up to the last moment, the two warders supporting the convict might stand securely holding him up, without danger to themselves or inconvenience to the machinery of the gallows. In this way Lamson was now kept erect while Marwood fastened his legs and put the cap over his eyes. Lamson pitifully begged that the chaplain may recite one more prayer.

Willing as the executioner possibly might have been to his request, of course he had no power to alter the progress of the service, and was obliged to disregard this last demand of the dying man.

Signalling to the warders to withdraw their arms, he drew the lever which released the bolt under the drop, and so launched the prisoner into eternity. The clergyman finished the Lord's Prayer, in the midst of which he found himself when the lever had been pulled, and then, pronouncing the benediction, moved slowly back to the prison. The body hung in place for an hour, in accordance with the law, after which it was taken down and placed in a shell coffin for the purpose of inspection.

During the afternoon Mr. G. H. Hull, one of the coroners for Surrey, held an inquest on the body of Lamson. Evidence as to the identity having been produced, Dr. Wyntner, the surgeon of Wandsworth Prison, stated that he examined the body of the deceased, and that death which had been instantaneous and painless, was due to apoplexy."

The Illustrated Police News produced one of their fine engravings to depict the scene on the gallows."

On May 16th, 1882, Marwood returned to Durham for the execution of Thomas Fury, alias Wright, alias Cutt, for the murder of Maria Fitzsimmons by stabbing her in the breast in a house in Baines Lane, Sunderland, on February 20th, 1869.

On February 19th, 1869, Maria, a prostitute who worked the docks at Sunderland, was seen drinking in the company of a sailor. Early next morning her body was found in her room; she had been stabbed ten times, nine of which had pierced her heart. A sailor called Anderson was arrested next day. Later that week a note was found which had been signed by 'A monster in human form.' The note claimed that Anderson was innocent and that its author was the real killer and on his way to America. With no real evidence against Anderson, the man was released and the case left unsolved despite someone offering one hundred pounds to catch the killer. Ten years later, in the spring of 1879, Thomas Fury, aka Wright, also a sailor, was arrested on a charge of burglary and attempted murder at Norwich. Soon after his arrest, he enquired whether the reward offered for information on the killing of Maria Fitzsimmons could still be claimed, as he said he could identify the killer. When told the reward was no longer available, he said no more about it. He was tried for the attempted murder and sentenced to fifteen years at Pentonville but no sooner had he started his sentence than he asked to see a police inspector and confessed that he had murdered Fitzsimmons. Fury said he'd awoken after spending the night with her, to find her attempting to strangle him with a cord. He knocked her down, pulled out his knife and stabbed her. He was taken back to Durham. Convicted at the summer Assizes to hang at the by Justice Williams, entirely on his own testimony and awaiting execution, he confided to a guard that he had confessed to the crime in order to escape the torture of a life inside the prison.

On May 22nd, Marwood was at Norwich Castle for the execution of William George Abigail who murdered

Mary Jane Plunkett. At 6am on Tuesday, April 25th, 1882, twenty-two year old Mary was found shot dead in the room she shared with Abigail. At the time Abigail worked as a waiter at the Star Hotel, Norwich and it was there where he first met Plunkett, a chambermaid. She didn't tell Abigail she was already married and later they went through a form of marriage. They moved in with his half-brother at New Catton. It was the son of Abigail's brother who reported hearing the shots to the police. Jane Plunkett was discovered blasted in the head and chest. Abigail confessed that he had killed her when he found out she was already married. He was tried, convicted and executed in Norwich on May 22nd, 1882. The next day, Marwood was at Leeds Armley Gaol for the execution of Osmond Otto Brand for the murder of William Pepper.

Marwood's next execution took place at Liverpool on August 21st, 1882, where he executed William Turner who murdered his wife at Skelmersdale.

The Times newspaper the following day states:

"Execution at Liverpool."

"William Turner was yesterday hanged within the precincts of the prison at Kirkdale, Liverpool, for the murder of his wife on June 23rd. The couple had been married for twenty years, and the man had been greatly addicted to drink. On the date mentioned he deliberately put on his boots and kicked her in a horrible manner. The poor woman, who was already ill and crippled, shrieked out, "Oh, Will, don't kill me as thou hast near done many a time." Another woman also begged of Turner to desist, but he threatened to serve her in the same way. Only the prison officials were present at the execution. The governor states that the culprit maintained a demeanour of composure and fortitude to the last."

At his shop on September 11th, Marwood received a letter from the governor of Exeter prison telling him he was preparing a new place for executions and wished to know the height of the beam from the platform and how deep the well under the drop should be. Marwood answered the letter when he came back from his next execution.

On September 11th, 1882, Marwood was in Limerick, Ireland, for the execution of Francis Hynes who murdered John Doloughty, an old shepherd. Doloughty was a father of seven who was employed as a herdsman on an evicted farm (farm taken over by the owner after none payment of rent) at Moyresik, two miles from Ennis, County Clare. On July 9th, Doloughty went into Ennis to attend lunchtime mass and as he walked home he was ambushed and shot in the chest and head. The shot had blown away both his eyes. A passer-by discovered the body and as he looked around for any clues he heard a rustle in the bushes and recognised Hynes, who fired at him but only managed to inflict minor wounds. Other passers-by managed to detain the gunman until the police arrived. It was thought the crime was committed because Doloughty worked on the evicted farm and that Hynes was sympathetic to the evicted man's plight. He had been one of a gang who had recently destroyed some property on the land. Mr Justice Lawson sentenced Hynes to death on August 12th.

This extract is from the newspaper 'The Clare Record' September 12th, 1882.

"The execution of Francis Hynes"

"Yesterday morning Francis Hynes paid the highest penalty that the law imposes, for the murder of the unfortunate Doloughty, near Ennis, on the 9th of July last. The morning was one of the finest which came for the past year - a fine glorious sunshine, a bright unclouded sky - all was warm and beautiful as our representative wended his way towards the County Gaol, where the culprit lay awaiting execution. From the appearance that the City presented at six o'clock in the morning the visitor would not imagine that in two short hours from that time, a young man, of splendid physique, full of youth and health would be done to death at the hands of the public executioner. But notwithstanding appearances, the fact was that Francis Hynes would at 8 o'clock, be executed by Marwood. As our reporter approached the County prison, a small knot of the lower classes were collected on the footway opposite the upper end of the gaol, while doubled sentries walked round the square, which the outer walls of the prison form. On the roads encircling the gaol fifteen constables, under the command of Constable Kavanagh, were on duty. The utmost precautions were observed by the authorities to ensure the safe keeping of the prisoner, and the due execution of the sentence of death which had been passed upon him. At about 6.15 am eight men of the 70th Regiment marched into the precincts of the gaol with loaded rifles and bayonets fixed, and in a short time afterwards a large body of constabulary, under the command of Sub-Inspector

Henry Wilton and Head Constables Rolleston and Phelan, and accompanied by Mr Bourke Irwin, Resident Magistrate, who had command of the troops and police, marched from William Street barracks and halted in front of the main entrance to the prison. As the police marched to the prison the military guard turned out and presented arms. The main body of the constabulary were then marched into the prison, while two parties patrolled the road outside.

At 7 o'clock crowds of people commenced to flock towards the gaol, and half an hour subsequently there were over a thousand persons present. The majority of the persons attending were of the lowest classes from the dens of the City, from the reeking cellars, and the dark alleys and nameless haunts. They came in all their repulsiveness and wretchedness for the purpose of gratifying a morbid feeling of curiosity and being near the scene of the execution of a fellow creature. But to their credit be it said there was a total absence of profanity and obscenity which formerly disgraced public executions when the full tide of life eddied and poured in rapid currents through the streets to witness an execution. The demeanour of the crowd yesterday was exceptionally good, and nothing was heard but prayers for the future happy state of the prisoner who was about to be executed. The most wretched and debased creature present had an anxious look on his countenance and there was a solemnity in the perfect silence that reigned supreme that told well for these poor people.

Marwood arrived in Limerick by the 1.30 mail train on Saturday morning and was escorted by a guard of constabulary to the County Gaol where he has since remained. Marwood is a man of about five feet seven inches tall, slight build, sharp features and eyes restless in their gaze. He is an enthusiast in his profession which he states he has made a science of, and the persons whom he executed have no pain whatever. To use his own words" "I have studied my profession that a man dies at my hands with as little pain as I give myself by touching the back of my hand with my finger." At 5 o'clock young Hynes rose and dressed himself with scrupulous care in a borrowed tweed suit. He ate a hearty breakfast and appeared to be in good spirits, considering the awful fate which was so soon and so suddenly to overtake him. He was a man of about twenty-three years of age, six feet three inches in height, of athletic appearance, well made and had very handsome features, and was entirely unlike a man who would be guilty of the foul deed for which he was to suffer death. He conversed freely with the warders who were constantly with him in his cell, and remarked yesterday morning: "I don't care what they do with my body, but may God have mercy on my soul." His demeanour while in the custody of the Governor was a model of propriety and his manners to the ministrations of the Roman Catholic chaplain was marked by a sincerity which was becoming to his position.

At 7.30am the Sheriff for the County Clare entered the condemned cell and informed the unfortunate man that his hour was come, and in about five minutes afterwards Marwood appeared and pinioned the prisoner. The chaplain who had been with him since an early hour, and who appeared to be deeply affected, then handed the culprit a crucifix which he devoutly kissed. At 8.15am a procession was formed, two Roman Catholic clergymen leading and repeating the litany of the dead. Next followed the doomed man with a warder on each side. He walked firmly with his head erect and his eyes intently gazing on the crucifix, and his voice in response to the prayers of the clergymen "Lord have mercy on us, Christ have mercy on us" was clear and distinct, and yet marked with a religious awe and fervour. Then followed the Governor, and Deputy governor of the gaol, the Sheriff of the County Clare, and then Marwood. In that order the procession moved at a slow pace, the chaplain saying the prayers for the dead, the convict articulating the responses in a clear voice without a tremulous note. His bearing was firm and dignified, and without ostentation or bravado, winning the sympathy and approbation of everyone who beheld him, and subsequently called forth from the lips of Marwood feeling words of sorrow at the untimely end of such a fine looking young man. The sentries ceased their walk, and the other lookers-on at the dread spectacle stood aside with tears in their eyes, with heads bowed in sorrow, and a deep momentous silence prevailed. Not a lip moved, the bystanders barely breathed as the solemn voice of a priest repeating the litany of the dead was heard, and the head of the procession became visible.

The convict was deadly pale; his eyes wandering alternately from the clergymen to the body of soldiers and constabulary who were drawn up in the courtyard of the prison, and then he would lift his eyes to heaven and his lips send forth a solemn prayer to the almighty God. A partition running parallel to the inner wall hid the scaffold from the unfortunate man, who, as he approached it, seemed to endeavour to pierce the structure. After a lapse of fifteen minutes this partition was reached by the head of the procession, and the door in the structure was thrown open. The drop was reached by a short stair which the convict ascended with firm step. From a crossbeam descended the treacherous rope, and under this was placed the unfortunate man. The clergymen still performed their religious duties, and still the voice of the convict was heard in response.

Then Marwood stepped forward, placed the noose around the condemned man's neck, pulled a thin white cap over his ashen face, and then stooped and tied his feet securely together. The pinioning of the arms allowed his hands to clasp his crucifix. Marwood was then seen to leave the presence of the convict, who stood for a moment before the persons present. The bolt was drawn and Francis Hynes was launched into another world. A black flag was hoisted on the prison tower denoting that the execution had been carried out. Marwood afterwards remarked: "I never executed a finer man, nor a man with so much nerve. He walked to his doom with the utmost composure and I cannot but admire him." The chaplain who attended him in his last moments afterwards appealed to the congregation in St John's Cathedral to pray for the soul of Francis Hynes, who, he believed, died innocent of the crime for which he was convicted. Still more convincing is the hint in Marwood's own complimentary remarks, altogether out of character that he believed in the innocence of Hynes. Marwood left Limerick for the last time in the same manner in which he entered - by the back door. The covered mail van was again brought into requisition to convey him to the deserted platform of Boher Station to catch the night mail train to Dublin."

On September 22nd, 1882, Marwood was back in Galway, Ireland, for the execution of Patrick Walsh who murdered Martin Lyden. When the Walsh family was evicted from a farmhouse in Letterfrack, County Galway, the new tenants, Martin Lyden and his father John, reckoned without Republican vengeance. On April 24th, 1881, a group of armed men went to the farmhouse, took the Lydens outside and shot them. The old man John died instantly; the son Martin died a month later. Police immediately suspected Walsh and found the murder weapon at his new home. He was hanged on Friday, September 22nd, 1882, at Galway Prison. Before Marwood left the gaol the governor enquired if he was available to carry out further executions on December 15th, and what his charges would be.

On November 13th, 1882, Marwood was in Bodmin, Cornwall, for the execution of William Meager Bartlett who murdered his bastard daughter and on November 28th, Marwood was at York Castle for the execution of Edward Wheatfill who murdered sixteen-year old Peter Hughes.

On December 4th, 1882, Marwood was at Liverpool Kirkdale for the execution of nineteen-year old Bernard Mullarky who murdered Thomas Cruise.

Mullarky, Cruise and Tom Jordan, were three labourers employed on a farm owned by a John Sumner, where they were allowed to sleep in a hayloft. During the summer, Mullarky was heard to make repeated threats to Cruise, and one witness reported hearing him say that he would "Burn the place down and hang for Cruise." On Monday September 25th, a serious fire destroyed the hayloft and when it had burnt itself out, police found Cruise's body among the remains. The police ascertained that a blow to the head had killed Cruise before the fire started. Mullarky was immediately under suspicion and was later charged with murder, convicted and executed at Maghull, Liverpool, on December 4th.

On December 12th, 1882, Marwood was at Wandsworth for the execution of Charles Taylor who murdered his wife Caroline.

This report from The Times states:

"He was tried at the Old Bailey and pleaded that he was insane, a neighbour gave evidence - my name is Henry Denninhton. I live at 2, Tustin Street, Old Kent Road, and am a fishmonger, the prisoner lived in the sume house as me, with his wife Caroline Elizabeth and his two children they occupied the shop and parlour behind it on the ground-floor, and a bedroom upstairs. on "Wednesday afternoon, August 18th, about 3.30, I was in my sitting-room on the first-floor, having my dinner when I heard screams and ran downstairs. I saw the prisoner's daughter Caroline in the passage by the parlour door. I spoke to her, and she opened the parlour-door and I went in and saw the prisoner in the act of cutting his own throat, and his wife was lying by the side of him; he was lying almost close to her, leaning on his elbow—I saw he had something in his hand, but I cannot tell what it was I saw no more; I left and called for help; the police and the doctor came soon afterwards. I had never heard any quarrels between the prisoner and his wife, he was generally on affectionate terms with his wife until within a few weeks ago when, the old people came up, and after that, for the last seven weeks, they seemed to be on bad terms. I think he was on affectionate terms with his two daughters, and was very happy with them. I was very much surprised at what had occurred, he was a very strange man all through the time he was living in the same house as us.

The doctor gave evidence;-. "I am a surgeon in practice in the Old Kent Road, on Friday, 18th, August, I went to Tustin Street, between 3.30 and 4 o'clock, in the back room behind the shop I saw the prisoner and his wife on the floor the woman was quite dead when I arrived; with her throat cut. The cut extended from two inches behind the left ear, right across the side of the neck in front, and an inch beyond the centre of the throat, at the right side it was only a skin cut, very superficial, before that it had severed the jugular vein and the carotid artery and the muscles, considerable force must have been used as if a knife had been used by somebody from behind and drawn right across it would account for the injury I saw. I came to the conclusion it was not a self-inflicted wound, from its severity, and because it went so far back, she died from loss of blood from the wound. I examined the prisoner and he had a wound on his throat about four inches long, almost immediately underneath the jaw, it had slightly cut the windpipe, but not sufficiently deep to sever the large arteries, there was not very much bleeding from that. I think that was a self-inflicted wound, he complained of the cold. I attended to him, and next day ordered him to be removed to the hospital. Once or twice a week, from the end of August until he left the hospital, about three weeks ago, I spoke to the prisoner, to ascertain the state of his mind the opinion was partially formed from that opinion that. a man may be sane on some matters and insane on others—a partial insanity may exist—violent suspicion is a common symptom of insanity, but not a decisive test. The jury took just fifteen minutes to find him guilty and he was sentenced to death by hanging." He was executed on December 12th, 1882.

On December 15th, 1882, Marwood's last execution of the year took place in Galway, Ireland. It was a triple execution of Myles Joyce, Patrick Joyce and Patrick Casey for the murders of John Joyce and family.

This report came from The Irish Times newspaper states:

"They call Maamtrasna, a wild, rugged part of County Galway at the foot of Lough Mask, "Joyce Country." The Joyce's who lived there had nothing to do with James Joyce, the celebrated author of Ulysses, but it seems likely they were familiar with the father of William Joyce – who became the notorious Lord Haw-Haw, employed by the Nazis as a propagandist, and who was forced out of the area by Republicans in 1922, for helping the police. For centuries the Joyce's of Maamtrasna were split between those who followed the Loyalist line and those who followed the Republican agenda. The sporadic violence that broke out around their political quarrels finally exploded on the night of August 17th, 1882, when a Republican branch of the family murdered five Joyce's, all Loyalists. John Joyce, 45, was shot dead. His wife Bridget, 40, his mother Peggy, 85, daughter Peggy, 17, and son Michael, 17, were beaten to death with coshes, iron bars and various other weapons. Another son, aged 12, survived the attack and identified the attackers. But the police had already guessed who they were, and they quickly traced the outrage back to another murder, that had occurred eight months earlier when Republicans murdered two bailiffs. Three suspects were subsequently arrested – they would be hanged the following year. Loyalist John Joyce had helped the police to identify the bailiffs' Republican killers, and eventually the Republican Joyce's found out. Thirteen 'Joyce's' were tried for the 'Maamtrasna Massacre,' as it came to be called, at a special court in Dublin in November 1882. Eight were sentenced to death including five who pleaded guilty and were subsequently reprieved. Two died in prison during their long custodial sentences and the other three served 20 years before being released. The three 'Joyce's' who were hanged went to the gallows in Galway Prison on Friday, December 15th, 1882, in what was to be Ireland's last triple hanging. Miles Joyce died in agony, when Marwood, was obliged to push him down by the shoulders to complete the drop."

A correspondent of the Sheffield Telegraph described an interview he had with Marwood after the execution at his residence in Horncastle:

"Now, sir, will you take a seat, sir, and say what you require of me?" said my host, as he bowed out with profuse politeness a caller who was still with him at the hour of my appointment. "And before we go any further," he continued, "it might be as well to give me your name. I didn't quite catch it when you were here before." Having to this little extent satisfied the requirement of my entertainer he fell to business. "Now, what do you want to know? What can I tell you about Ireland? Have you been to Galway?"

I replied that I knew the city well, and told him the story of how a chief magistrate had once found his own son guilty of murder on the high seas, and not only sentenced him to death but as the story goes, hanged him with his own hand. "The chief magistrate did you say?" interposed my host. "Yes, the warden of Galway, a great man," and then I told him the whole tale of how James Lynch Fitz-Stephen sent his only son to Spain on commercial business, and found out some time afterwards that, returning with a Spanish friend, he conspired with the crew to throw the Spaniard overboard and seize for his own use a valuable cargo. After many months, stricken with horror, one of the crew revealed the circumstances. The young man was tried before his own father, was found guilty and sentenced to death. But the people of the town waited upon the mayor, and, depending party upon the fact that the young man was an only son, pleaded that his sentence should be commuted. 'You shall have my answer if you will call at midday to-morrow,' said the warden, calmly, and the deputation went away in good hope. Next day when they went to the house they found the body of the young man suspended from one of the front windows. This was the answer of the stern warden of Galway to the appeal for mercy." "A splendid fellow," said Marwood. "I should have done the same myself. If I can only get some of them to go with me I shall have a look at his house when I go back to Galway in the beginning of the year." From this time the tongue of my entertainer was loosened. He felt on quite the same mental plane as the Historical Mayor of Galway, and began benignly to give me his experiences.

I interrupted him by putting the question plainly whether it was or not a fact that in the case of Myles Joyce there was something so far wrong that the rope had to be adjusted by the executioners foot. "What have you seen in the papers?" He asked. And I showed him the story as told in a semi-local publication. The passage was as follows; - All the time Casey and Patrick Joyce remained unmoveable on the drop, and even when the white cap was drawn over their heads their firmness did not desert them. When Myles Joyce underwent the same ordeal he paused for a moment, but, as if unable to restrain himself, he again broke forth into words, and even as the lever was moved and the bolt drawn he was still speaking, and died with a protestation of innocence on his lips.

The strain upon the beam as the three men dropped was intense, and the dull thud and vibration of the cords was distinctly heard a considerable distance off the space. Beneath the drop was all boxed in, so that the bodies instantly dropped out of view. They were scarcely down when Marwood was observed to catch the rope on which Myles Joyce was suspended, and to put down his foot as if to disentangle or rearrange it. This he continued doing for a couple or three minutes, and the operation whatever it was, gave him some trouble, for once he ejaculated distinctly enough to be heard by the reporter "Bother the fellow." "That's not true," said Marwood. "Those Irish newspapers tell such lies."

"But reporters as a rule tell the truth" I interrupted. With a regard for the dignity of the profession, 'The Recording Angel' stated that you did stoop down and did say, "Bother the fellow." Is that true?"

The man looked a little confused, but answered with more promptness than I expected, "Well, yes; I believe I did say so. You see the fellow was so bothersome. Neither the priest nor me could make him stand. And he threw himself about so, across his breast, you know when they stand patient and properly it always lies loose on their shoulders and just before they drop, and when I looked down the pit was hanging crosswise like. His head was a little to one side, owing to the rope being caught in the arm, he did not hang straight like the other two. But he did not suffer anything, anymore than the others. He was a wild, bad looking fellow, and kept jabbering and talking. I couldn't understand a word of his 'lingo,' and I don't think the priest knew much of it, for he seemed frightened. But there was enough force of the rope on his neck to finish him in very little time. He was dead as soon as the others, though the doctors said he was 'strangulated.' I looked myself, and did see that his neck was not broken."

Chapter Twelve – Executions 1883

The first execution of 1883 took place at Maidstone on January 2nd. Marwood was there to execute Louisa Jane Taylor who murdered Mrs Mary Ann Tregellis. Taylor was an attractive thirty-seven year old woman who was hanged for the poisoning of eighty-two-year-old Mrs. Tregellis at Plumstead in Kent. Louisa had been widowed in 1882, and had a small pension. To help make ends meet, she took a live-in job as a nurse to the wife of a friend of her former husband, William Tregellis. His wife, Mary Ann, was in poor health, so it was agreed that Louisa would share her room while William would move into the front room. The Tregellis' soon started to notice things going missing from the house and were also dismayed that Mary Ann's health continued to deteriorate. Soon after Louisa's arrival, Mary Ann began to have fits and attacks of vomiting. The family doctor repeatedly tried to get Louisa to retain a sample of the vomit for analysis but she had always conveniently forgotten to do so. Dr Smith was at the same time prescribing 'sugar of lead' (lead acetate) to Louisa, which she claimed to be taking to improve her complexion. It appears not to have occurred to Dr. Smith that Mary Ann was being poisoned or that it was indeed he who was supplying the poison. On October 6th, 1882, William called the police to the house as his pension money had gone missing after Louisa took it from him, supposedly to give it to Mary Ann. She was later seen leaving the house by the Tregellis' landlady with the money in her hand. Dr. Smith was at the house when the police arrested Louisa and it finally dawned on him what had being going on. The frail old woman was in a terrible state and her gums showed the tell tale sign of lead poisoning when he examined them: a dark blue line at their edge. It was too late to save Mary Ann's life, however, and she died on October 23rd, 1882. An autopsy revealed large quantities of lead in her system and as Louisa, was already in custody, she was charged with the murder. She came to trial in December 1882. Her motive for the killing may have been financial but equally may have been the sadistic pleasure of watching Mary Ann die slowly from lead poisoning. The financial gain from killing Mary Ann could have been small at best, as the Tregellis' were quite poor and lived only on William's pension. One is left with the alternative motive: that she did it for pleasure and the ability to wield the power of life and death over another person. Louisa Jane Taylor was the last woman to be executed at Maidstone Gaol.

Marwood spent ten days in Ireland, in Galway and Tralee, for five executions. The first three took place in

Galway one on January 15th, and the other two on the 17th.

A report from The Irish Times states:

"Patrick Higgins, at a special sitting of the Dublin Special Commission, was convicted of the murder of Joseph and John Huddy at Clougbrack, Lough Mask, on January 3rd, 1882. The two men were bailiffs employed by Lord Ardilaun. They were requested to evict Higgins and his family from a farm they rented on the Lord's land after they fell behind with the payments. As the bailiffs called at the farm, Patrick Higgins and his two accomplices attacked the men. Patrick attacked Joseph Huddy with a stone and knocked him down, while Thomas Higgins shot dead the younger Huddy. The three accused men then forced witnesses at gunpoint to assist them in tying up the two men and to carry the bodies to Lough Mask. The bodies were later found chained together under a spur near the Lough."

Patrick Higgins, his accomplices, Michael Flynn and Thomas Higgins were found guilty of the murders of Joseph and John Huddy. Marwood executed Patrick Higgins on January 15th, and Michael Flynn and Thomas Higgins on January 17th.

From Galway Marwood went to Tralee for a further two executions on January 23rd. The persons he executed were Thomas Barratt and Sylvester Poff who murdered Thomas Brown.

A report from The Irish Times states:

"Hangman Marwood was the target for a mob of more than one thousand angry Irishmen when he arrived at Limerick railway station to hang these two killers. The locals were convinced that Sylvester Poff and Thomas Barrett were innocent of killing Thomas Brown who had been shot dead in broad daylight on his farm at Dromoulton near Castleisland, County Kerry, in October 1882.

The principal prosecution witness, an old lady, said she saw the two men enter Brown's field, argue heatedly with him and then shoot him. The prosecution claimed that the motive was a dispute over land, which Poff and Barrett wanted to acquire for the Republican movement.

Carpenters were brought in from Dublin under police protection to build the scaffold, and after the execution Marwood was given an armed escort back to the station."

On February 12th, 1883, Marwood was in Manchester Strangeways Prison for the execution of Abraham Thomas who murdered housekeeper, Christina Leigh. Thomas was a butler in a large house on the outskirts of Bolton, owned by Captain Thomas Chester Andsell. On December 22nd, Andsell decided to spend Christmas and New Year at his daughter's home. Before he left he placed the housekeeper, Mrs Christina Leigh, in charge of the household. Relieved of his duties, Thomas decided to start his celebrations early and went to the local public house for some refreshment. He came home quite late and rather drunk. Mrs Leigh reprimanded Thomas the following morning about his behaviour. At this Thomas took offence.

After the New Year celebrations Andsell returned to the house and was told of Thomas's conduct. Andsell sacked Thomas telling him to leave the house immediately and never to return. The next day a gardener saw Thomas entering the gun store. The gardener told Mrs Leigh and she went to find Thomas. On entering the gun store a shot was heard. A housemaid went to investigate and saw Thomas, shotgun in hand, standing over Mrs Leigh's body. The police were called and he was arrested.

At his trial at the Manchester Assizes Thomas pleaded insanity but the prosecution proved otherwise as the matching gun was found in his quarters fully loaded. He was sentenced to death by Justice Key, hanged and buried afterwards within the prison walls.

On February 19th, Marwood was in Lincoln County Gaol for the execution of James Anderson who murdered his wife.

An article in the Lincoln Mercury states:

"In Lincoln on February 19th, 1883, fifty-year-old Anderson, a Lincolnshire coal miner was sentenced to death by Mr Justice Cave at Lincoln Assizes for the murder of his wife at Gainsborough on December 6th, 1882. Anderson had cut her throat and then his own, after a quarrel. He expressed deep regret for the crime at his trial and despite a petition signed by thousands of local people he was executed and buried within the prison grounds of Lincoln Castle."

On April 30th, Marwood was in Cork, Ireland for the execution of Timothy O'Keefe for the murder of his uncle John O'Keefe. Timothy O'Keefe was convicted at his second trial for the murder of his uncle, who was shot dead at Kingwilliamstown on Sunday, April 30th, 1882. At the first trial the jury had failed to agree, but at the second, the prosecution claimed there was evidence that proved the prisoner's guilt. They alleged that Timothy's father had financial difficulties and had to sell their farm. The uncle bought the farm and evicted his brother when he couldn't pay his debts. The execution was originally scheduled for April 26th, but it had to be put back as Marwood was otherwise engaged. When Marwood eventually carried out the execution he gave O'Keefe a drop of nine feet due to O'Keefe's height and light weight.

On May 7th, Marwood was back in Lincoln for the execution of Thomas Garry who murdered John Newton. Garry was a labourer convicted of the murder of John who was a seventy-four-year-old farmer, residing at Great Hale Fen, Sleaford. Newton had lived alone on his farm since the death of his wife in the summer of 1882. Garry worked for him as a casual labourer and slept at the Newton's house. At the beginning of 1883, Garry took to drink resulting in his work becoming sloppy. He was given a warning by the old man, that if Garry didn't improve he would have to move on. On February 2nd, Newton was found dead on the kitchen floor in the farmhouse. He had been blasted in the chest with his own shotgun, which lay nearby. The Police came and found a bloodstained footprint which matched markings on Garry's boots, further examination revealed bloodstains on his clothing. He was tried and convicted at Lincolnshire Assizes and hanged on May 7th, 1883.

On May 8th, Marwood was in Chester for the execution of Patrick Carey who murdered Samuel

Carlam and Mary Mohan. Samuel and his common-law wife, Mary, kept a lodging house at Smallwood, a village just outside Congleton, Cheshire. On February 9th, they were found battered to death in the house, which had also been burgled. A hammer was found beside the bodies. The police soon learned that a tramp carrying a large bundle had been seen in the area shortly after the robbery was discovered. Police arrested Patrick Carey, a father of four, and also known as John White. He was tried and convicted at Chester Assizes and sentenced to death. Marwood hanged Carey in Chester on May 8th, 1883. It was the last execution held in the city.

Marwood's next two executions were at Dublin's Kilmainham Gaol, Ireland. Joseph Brady, Daniel Curley, Thomas Caffrey, Timothy Kelly and Michael Fagan had been sentenced to death for their part in what became known as 'The Phoenix Park Murders.'

On May 6th, 1882, Lord Frederick Cavendish, the British Secretary for Ireland and his under secretary, Thomas Henry Burke, two of the most senior officials in the British administration of Ireland, were strolling through Phoenix Park in Dublin, on their way to dinner. They were set upon by a group of men armed with surgical knives. Death was swift, silent, bloody and terrible. The attackers made their escape and although the killing took place in broad daylight, the authorities had no idea who had done the murders. It took nine months of painstaking detective work to put the case together. In January 1883, a number of men were arrested. They were members of 'The Invincibles,' which was a radical splinter group of the Irish Brotherhood. It is known that informers helped bring the gang to justice.

Jim Carey, a prominent figure in 'The Invincibles' struck a deal with the authorities and turned Queen's evidence. This resulted in the five men being sentenced to death and others being sentenced to long prison terms. Carey was sent to South Africa for his own safety. Although his trip was planned in great secrecy, he was murdered on board the ship. His killer Patrick O'Donnell was hanged in England in December 1883, by Marwood's successor Bartholomew Binns. Marwood executed Joseph Brady on May 14th.

An account of the last moments of Joe Brady from The Irish Times states:

"When Marwood was to perform the first operation of pinioning he found Brady resigned to his fate. It was just a quarter to eight when the executioner shook him by the hand. The pinioning of the arms was quickly effected and Marwood hurried on to the scaffold and adjusted the rope hanging from the crossbeam. When Brady entered the yard his eyes glanced swiftly at the structure and climbed the incline to the platform and stepped on the trap door. He looked round at the few spectators and smiled slightly by way of farewell, with a gesture from Marwood he stepped a little forward as to come almost directly under the rope. With rapidity the executioner clasped the leather straps round Brady's lower limbs. In a second the cap was placed over his face and the noose of rope was placed around his neck. Marwood gave one hurried but searching look to the beam above, touches the lever close to his side – the floor gives way beneath the feet of Brady – his body disappears like a flash from view – a heavy thud is heard and all is still and silent as the grave. Death was instantaneous."

On May 18th, Marwood was back at Kilmainham gaol to execute thirty-one-year-old Daniel Curley. Thirty-one-year-old Curley a Superintendent within 'The Invincibles' was alleged to have master minded the murders in Phoenix Park. When the drop fell his death was instantaneous. Marwood was to return to Ireland later to execute the other persons.

On May 21st, 1883, Marwood was in Taunton for two executions. The first was Joseph Wedlake, who murdered Mark Cox and the second George White. The latter murdered his wife, Clara, by kicking her to death less than twelve months after they married. White pleaded guilty at the Taunton Assizes, never attempting to deny his offence.

This report came from the Taunton Journal:

"Wedlake was jealous of a young man named Thatcher, who was courting his cousin Emma Pearce. On Sunday night, January 7th, he lay in wait of Thatcher with the intention of killing him with an axe. But Wedlake mistook Cox for his intended victim and killed him. Wedlake's brother, who had been arrested for the crime, revealed the facts to the police and Joseph confessed.

Both prisoners, having given up all hope of a reprieve, walked firmly to the gallows that had been erected in a room at the end of a corridor in the gaol. Death was instantaneous. Before the execution, a bell was tolled and afterwards, a black flag was raised above the gaol."

On May 23rd, Marwood was in Glasgow for the double execution of Henry Mullen and Martin Scott who had murdered two gamekeepers. This was Marwood's last visit to Glasgow before his death.

On May 28th, Marwood returned to Ireland for the executions of Michael Fagan, Thomas Caffrey and Timothy Kelly. At Dublin's Kilmainham Gaol on May 28th, Marwood executed Michael Fagan and on June 2nd, he executed Thomas Caffrey. Marwood executed Timothy Kelly on June 9th, who at nineteen-years-of-age was the youngest of the condemned. All three of the executed men were involved in the murders in Phoenix Park. There was a feeling of commiseration for Kelly on account of his age and up to the last moment of his life there were hopes that he might be reprieved.

Marwood's last execution took place in Durham on August 6th, 1883, where he executed a bigamist, James Burton for the murder of his eighteen-year-old wife, Elizabeth Sharp, whom he had married whilst he already had a wife and family.

This extract from the Sunderland Echo states:

"The arrival of an elderly man at the Dun Cow pub in Durham on the night of Saturday, August 4th, 1883, would probably have caused something of a stir.

The man Marwood had come to hang was James Burton, a 38-year-old labourer from Sunderland convicted of the murder of his 17-year-old wife, Elizabeth.

The couple had met the previous summer, while both ill in Sunderland Infirmary.

They married at Sunderland Register Office and set up home in North Durham Street.

But there was something Burton had failed to tell his young sweetheart – he was already married. He had also suffered a severe head injury as a child, leaving him bad tempered. Matters were made worse when he gashed his hand in a shipyard accident. He was unable to work and began taking laudanum – a highly addictive mix of opium and alcohol. As the money ran out, so the couple began to argue. Eventually, after Burton tried to strangle Elizabeth she walked out and tried to rebuild her life. Burton began to stalk her however, and on May 8th, 1883, his obsession was to turn to tragedy. Elizabeth's body was later found lying near the railway track at Silksworth. The back of her head was smashed in and three large rocks were resting on top of her. Police were soon on the trail of Burton, eventually capturing him the next morning. He denied any knowledge of the murder, but bloodstains on his trousers and a blood-soaked woman's neckerchief told another story. Burton stood trial for murder at Durham Assizes on July 20th, he pleaded not guilty and claimed Elizabeth had been killed by a fall of rocks from the railway cutting.

Medical evidence, however, proved he was lying and he was found guilty and sentenced to be "hanged by the neck until he was dead" by the Judge Justice Hawkins. Marwood left the Dun Cow pub on the morning of August 8th, 1883, to walk to Durham Prison to carry out the execution. He estimated Burton would need a drop of about eight feet. As the prison clock chimed 8am, Marwood pulled the trap-door lever and Burton plunged into the pit."

Another account from a local newspaper states:

"The culprit walked firmly to the scaffold but on being placed in position looked up at the cross beam and on those assembled around the scaffold. Marwood the executioner at once placed the white cap over the culprit's face, fastened his legs and fixed the rope. Immediately the bolt was drawn it was obvious something had gone wrong, the body was swinging violently to and fro in the pit. Marwood seized hold of the rope and assisted by two warders, dragged the still living man out of the pit. When drawn up Burton presented a shocking appearance. As Marwood went to pull the lever, Burton fainted and began to fall sideways, his pinioned arms catching in the loop of the rope hanging down his back, thus prevented him dropping properly. The noose had also slipped up over Burton's chin. Marwood and the warders now had to get the poor man back onto the platform to disentangle him and having done so, Marwood pushed him off the side of the trap. He swayed back and forth struggling for a couple of minutes before unconsciousness supervened. His face was badly contorted and his neck very swollen when the coroner's jury at the formal inquest viewed his body later in the day, it was clear that he had strangled to death. It was stated that whist the rope was being adjusted the second time the victim muttered twice "Oh, Lord, have mercy on my poor soul!"

Burton, prior to his execution had written to the parents of his victim a full confession of his crime. In the letter he states that they had a quarrel while walking up a lane in Tunstall. He put out his hand to give her a note she had dropped when she screamed and poked him in the chest with her umbrella. She threatened to fetch her brother Henry, and said she would swear his life away, and again poked him with her umbrella. "Then" wrote Burton, "my temper got the best of me, and I struck her, and we both fell. She got up first, and asked me not to hit her any more. At that time I could not see out of my eyes for tears, and she cried out, 'Oh, Jim Burton! I'm only trying you. Don't hit me any more; ' and I said, 'It is too late now, for I have not a home for myself.' I was blind at the time with passion, and I picked up a stone and hit her with it, and she fell down in the same place where her body was picked up. Then she said, 'Jim, don't for the last time do come with me Jim.' Then after I had seen what I had done, I placed the stones on her that were lying alongside her. Burton then described how he watched at the scene of the murder until he saw the body taken up by railway men, and how he wandered about for several days, making more than one attempt to poison himself with laudanum. He expressed much penitence for his crime."

On the Thursday after the execution, a Horncastle reporter had an interview with Marwood, with regard to the incident that happened at the execution. Marwood stated the facts were quite different from the criticisms of the newspapers of the north and said that they had exaggerated the mishap, which he acknowledged had occurred. "Some of the reporters," he added, "have their knives in me," but he also stated, "he would sooner have reporters present as not, as he was willing to meet them all as long as they write the truth."

Marwood asserted that there had never been a bungle on his part at an execution yet. Referring to Monday's execution, Marwood explained everything was well arranged, as at other times. The culprit Burton walked from his cell with a weak step, and was duly pinioned and placed on the drop. The noose was properly fixed, but as Marwood went towards the lever Burton fainted and fell backwards. When Burton fell his left elbow was caught in the slack of the rope; but this did not occur until after the lever had been pulled, and without delay Burton was raised to the edge of the pit, and Marwood removed the rope from his elbow instantly, letting him fall again into the pit below. Dislocation of the neck took place immediately. If Burton had not fainted no incident would have occurred. Marwood emphatically denied that the noose slipped on to the face of Burton. "It never moved an inch from where it was placed" said Marwood "and it never had to be adjusted."

Questioned as to his opinion of the system, by the reporter. Marwood affirmed that it was the most humane and the quickest in the whole world. As to the insinuations of being drunk, Marwood declared that it was quite false, as he had only had a cup of tea that morning. The statement that his ropes had been exhibited on the previous Sunday is a false one as well. Marwood stated they were never seen by anyone in Durham till the Monday when they were placed on the gallows. Referring to the charge of him parading the streets with the same pride as a victorious army general, and refusing private quarters in the prison Marwood again stated "that was far from the truth." The reporter stated "he understood that there was no accommodation for him at the gaol, so he went to a hotel." Marwood said, "that was right and until the time of the execution I never left the hotel. The prison is the fitted place for me to stay in." He also said, "I always stay in the gaol, if I am allowed."

Burton's bungled death caused a scandal and questions were raised in the House of Commons. MPs were told Marwood had also made mistakes during a hanging in Galway. The Sunderland Echo tightened the noose still further, suggesting Marwood had been drunk, commenting: "If Marwood makes boots as badly as he hangs murderers, it is no wonder that he has had to turn an extra pound or two by acting as crown officer, and that this disaster was the finish of Marwood." Marwood was brought before the authorities and relieved of his duties, pending an inquiry. On the way home Marwood got a bad cold.

Four weeks later, on Tuesday September 4th, 1883, the Editor of The Illustrated Police News received a telegram from The Central News reporter at Horncastle the wording was as follows:

"Marwood died here at two o'clock this afternoon of congestion of the lungs and jaundice. He was, at the time of his decease, sixty-three years of age.(sic) He had held office a little over ten years."

Idle rumour had it that Marwood had been poisoned by Irish sympathisers whilst sharing a few drinks in his Horncastle local, The Portland Arms, as revenge for executing the 'Phoenix Park' murderers. When going over to Ireland Marwood was always very chatty with his fellow passengers, who were generally unaware of his identity.

On October 6th, Marwood's wife, Elen, received a letter from Madame Tussaud's requesting William's last suit of clothes, which they stated he had promised to give them at his last sitting. It appears that they were in the process of making a new model of him before he died.

Elen survived Marwood by only three months, dying in December 1883. In this time she sold his clothes to Madame Tussaud's and the ropes to Mr. James Harrison of Dispey Road, Horncastle, who was not disposed to split his new collection.

Since the Marwood's had no surviving children all their possessions were auctioned - including his dog, Nero.

Marwood had done well out of his shoe making business, after a lifetime of relative poverty in the early days. It was said at his death that he owned several cottages. A sale of Marwood's effects took place at Horncastle on November 6th, 1883. One of his ropes was sold for ninety shillings and his Gladstone bag went for sixty shillings.

Marwood's body was interred on September 6th, 1883, in the graveyard attached to the Holy Trinity Chapel of Ease on Spilsby Road, Horncastle. Over the years curio-seekers chipped away at his gravestone and took fragments until there was nothing left of it.

There had been delays in winding up the affairs of Marwood after his death, caused by a difficulty as to the legal heir.

However, after more than two years after his death, on November 28th, 1885, the Horncastle News and South Lindsey Advertiser carried the following notice:

"William Marwood deceased, all persons having any Claim or Demand against the Estate or Effects of William Marwood, late of Horncastle, in the County of Lincoln, cordwainer, deceased, who died on the September 4th 1883, are requested forthwith to send the particulars therefore to me, the undersigned, the solicitor for Mr James Isle, a creditor of the said deceased. Robert Clitherow, Solicitor."

On April 11th 1890, another notice appeared as follows:

"The Bankruptcy Act, 1883."

"In Bankruptcy, Re William Marwood, deceased. Notice is hereby given, that an Order was made by the County Court of Lincolnshire, holden at Lincoln on the 26th day of February 1890 for the Administration in Bankruptcy of the Estate of William Marwood, late of Horncastle, in the county of Lincoln, cordwainer, deceased, and the Official Receiver of the said Court was appointed the Trustee. Notice is also hereby given that a meeting of the creditors of the said William Marwood deceased will be held at the office 31 Silver Street, Lincoln, on 17th, April. R. J. Ward, Official Receiver." After everything was settled Marwood was declared bankrupt at his death for the miserly sum of £31. 6s. 4d.

There was much surprise, especially in Horncastle, that Marwood had died insolvent. It was assumed that he had accumulated a considerable sum of money. He had a thriving cobbling business, received regular earnings as an executioner, and had bought quite a number of properties. It is presumed his investments did not turn out well, and probably the agricultural depression at the time was responsible for his insolvency.

After his death in 1883 his home 64, Foundary Street and shop 6, Church Lane became important landmarks in Horncastle. On the August 30th, 1990, a picture of a cottage appeared in the local Horncastle newspaper with this report:

'The mysterious and historical 'Hangman's Cottage,' once owned by William Marwood, is now on the market awaiting offers by potential buyers. The two-roomed cottage is being handled by the local agents could be developed into a mews house by a prospective buyer, who could benefit from its central location of St Mary's Square. He was known for keeping the executioner's ropes in the premises."

The last boot and shoe repairer to occupy William Marwood's little cobbler's shop on Church Road was a man named Mr. Kirton.

Chapter Thirteen – Conclusion

The death of William Marwood created a vacancy for an executioner.

In Sepember 1883, George Watson, aged twenty-seven, wrote a letter to the Sheriff of York to replace the deceased William Marwood as executioner.

"Sir, To be forarded To the most grave and revent senior sherif of york i Georg Watson aply for the ofis of publick exectutner in place of the most reverd and late lamented mr marwood if your iness appoints me i will give satisfactshun to all parties conserned speshaly the unappy criminels which will now nowt if your iness appoint me promp tenshon like shal be my moto and a post mortal after as wil show the unappy criminels insensitif. if your iness wish i will com and visit yu for a few days like and explain my pricipl. As the guverment will have somat to sa wich is libral in this matter yu will elp me if you tel em i is a libral twas awful last ellectshun fittin agen downses all by myself like samy rowlanson will tell you ow he was were he was thro me and gladston likes a man like me kindred sperit like hoopin yu will give me a erly hanging for which yu wil be responible and your petitoneer will evur pray hoopin we may both life long and hang together."

In 1928 a gentleman named Hugh Kenyon of Surrey discovered this copy of the letter from George Watson in the office of the Under-Sheriff of Yorkshire.

George Watson, never got the position to replace Marwood.

William Marwood's successor was Bartholomew Binns. He was in office from 1883 until 1884 when he was sacked. Bartholomew Binns' first solo execution was Henry Powell on November 6th, 1883. After Powell's execution he started drinking heavily. Binns was reported several times for being drunk and being unable to calculate the length of the drop correctly. As a result a number of his convicts died in agony upon the scaffold. Binns last execution was that of Michael McLean on March 10th, 1884. It was reported that McLean took thirteen minutes to die.

Binns successor was James Berry, executioner from 1884 until 1891. He was the first British hangman to be literate enough to be able to write freely about his work. He was also the last to be allowed to do so. The most important contribution he made to the 'trade' was an amendment of the 'long drop' method developed by William Marwood.

Berry's improvements were intended to diminish mental and physical suffering and some of them remained standard practice until the abolition of capital punishment for murder. Berry's time in office came to an end following interference in his judgement by the prison medical officer at Kirkdale, regarding the appropriate length of drop; Berry compromised but the condemned man, John Conway, was nearly decapitated. In March 1892 Berry wrote out his letter of resignation, probably without knowing that in October of the previous year the Home Office had already decided that Berry, as executioner, should no longer be recommended to the High Sheriffs.

After Berry, there were numerous men employed as executioners including the Billington family and the Pierrepoint family. Britain's last hangman was Harry Allen assitant executioner from 1941 until 1955 and then chief executioner from 1957 until the suspension of capital punishment in 1965. He executed twenty nine culprits, as he liked to call them, as number one, and assisted at fifty three others. His last execution was in 1964. Capital punishment in Great Britain was abolished in 1969 and 1973 in Northern Ireland.

Everyone of Marwood's successors used with slight modification the 'long drop' tables which he developed way back in the year 1869. His tables of calculations were never really bettered.

Marwood's employment as exectioner was never terminated. Prior to his death in September 1883, he was temporary suspended from his duties whilst an investigation into the execution of James Burton was being carried out. But even as far back 1879 doubts were being raised about his claim to "guarantee instantaneous death." This passage is from a letter written to London Times in 1879:

"Sir, - subjoined is a list of criminals executed by Marwood, all of whom, according to the papers, showed signs of life in a greater or lesser after the drop fell. The convicts Stewart, Coates, Anderson, Deacon, Marks, Walker, Smart and Dilley were described as dying a particular painful death. Reference to the papers containing the accounts will, I believe, corroborate this statement:

Frances Stewart, executed June 29, 1874, at Newgate.

Robert Cranwell, executed Jan. 4, 1875, at Newgate.

Richard Coates, executed March 29, 1875, at Maidstone

Mark Fiddler, executed Aug. 16, 1875, at Lancaster

John Wm. Anderson, executed Dec. 22, 1875, at Newcastle

Edward Deacon, executed April 24, 1876, at Bristol

Richard Thompson, executed Aug. 14, 1876, at Kirkdale

Isaac Marks, executed Jan. 2, 1877, at Horsemonger Lane

John Goulding, executed Aug. 21, 1877, at Kirkdale

Patrick McGovern, executed Aug. 21, 1877, at Kirkdale

Vincent Knowles Walker, executed April 15, 1878, at York

Edwin Smart, executed May 12, 1879, at Bristol

James Dilly, executed Aug. 25, 1879, at Newgate

In justice to Marwood it may, however, be stated that in many cases criminals are described as dying instantaneously by his method of execution; and instances are not wanting of the hard death by means of the short drop; e.g. that of Goodwin, executed at Newgate on Whit Monday 1874, – the last time Calcraft officiated there."

Marwood was a deeply religious man who often knelt together with the condemned to ask God's blessing. He always said "I am doing God's work according to the divine command and the law of the British crown. I do it simply as a matter of duty and as a Christian. I sleep soundly as a child in my bed and never am disturbed by phantoms. When I get out of bed on the morning of an execution I kneel down quietly and ask God's blessing on the work I have to do, and ask mercy for the prisoner. I have a sense of divine mission and a belief that regardless of what deeds the condemned man has perpetrated in his time, he deserves to be dispatched as painless as possible."

Marwood's view of hanging was that capital punishment should never be abandoned.

"What would you substitute it with?" he was to say.

"If you send a man to penal servitude, a warden has to stand over him and you have to feed him, but hang him and he's done with. Nothing but hanging will prevent murders happening. Show them the gallows and they will think twice before they go ahead and commit crime. There is no better deterrent than hanging."

Marwood was convinced that the job of the executioner was necessary for the good of society. He was determined to carry it out in as decent and humane a manner as possible. He was known as an exhibitionist, but he always behaved as a perfect gentleman towards the condemned persons he was obliged to execute.

William Marwood, gentleman and executioner, would tap the condemned on the shoulder, shake them by the hand and say "Come along with me I shall not hurt you."

Appendix 1

The Official Table of Drops, published by the British Home Office is a manual used to calculate the correct length of rope for the long drop hangings. The weight is that of the clothed prisoner in pounds, the day before execution.

Body weight			1888-1913 drop		Modern drop	
Stone	lb	Kg	Ft	cm	Ft	cm
14.0	196	89	8 0"	244	5 5"	165
13.5	189	86	8 2"	249	5 6"	168
13.0	182	82¾	8 4"	254	5 8"	173
12.5	175	79½	8 6"	259	5 11"	180
12.0	168	76¼	8 8"	264	6 1"	185
11.5	161	73¼	8 10"	269	6 4"	193
11.0	154	70	9 0"	274	6 6"	198
10.5	147	66¾	9 2"	279	6 8"	203
10.0	140	63¾	9 4"	284	7 1"	215
9.5	133	60½	9 6"	290	7 5"	226
9.0	126	57¼	9 8"	295	7 7"	231
8.5	119	54	9 10"	300	7 9"	236
8.0	112	51	10 0"	305	8 0"	244

Appendix 2

Date Condemned		Place
1 April 1872	William Frederick Horry,	Lincoln
30 Dec 1872	Michael Kennedy	Manchester
4 Aug 1873	Benjamin Hudson	Derby
26 Aug 1873	Thomas Montgomery	Omagh
8 Sept 1873	James Connor	Liverpool
5 Jan 1874	Charles Dawson	Durham
	William Thompson
	Edward Gough
29 June 1874	Frances Stewart (F)	Newgate
10 Aug 1874	John Macdonald	Exeter
24 Aug 1874	James Henry Giggs	Usk
31 Aug 1874	Henry Flanagan	Liverpool
	Mary Williams (F)
13 Oct 1874	John Walter Coppen	Horsemonger
16 Nov 1874	Thomas Smith	Winchester
28 Dec 1874	Hugh Daley	Durham
29 Dec 1874	Robert Taylor	Stafford
4 Jan 1875	James Cranwell	Newgate
24 Mar 1875	John McDaid	Sligo
29 Mar 1875	Richard Coates	Chelmsford
30 Mar 1875	John Morgan	Maidstone
9 April 1875	John Russell	Clonmel
19 April 1875	Alfred Thomas Heap	Liverpool
26 April 1875	William Hale	Bristol
27 July 1875	Jeremiah Corkery	Warwick

2 Aug 1875	Michael Gillingham	Durham
	William McHugh	
	Elizabeth Pearson (F)	
9 Aug 1875	Peter Blanchard	Lincoln
11 Aug 1875	Joseph Le Brun	Jersey
16 Aug 1875	William McCullough	Lancaster
	Mark Fiddler	
6 Sept 1875	William Baker	Liverpool
	Edward Cooper	
5 Oct 1875	Patrick Docherty	Glasgow
19 Oct 1875	David Wardlaw	Dumbarton
21 Dec 1875	Henry Wainwright	Newgate
22 Dec 1875	John William Anderson	Newcastle
23 Dec 1875	Richard Charlton	Morpeth
28 Mar 1876	George Hunter	Morpeth
4 April 1876	Thomas Fordred	Maidstone
10 April 1876	George Hill	St Albans
24 April 1876	Edward Deacon	Bristol
25 April 1876	Joseph Webber	Cardiff
26 April 1876	John Daly	Belfast
23 May 1876	Giovanni Caccaris	Newgate
	Pascaler Caladis	
	Matteo Corgalis	
	George Kadi	
31 May 1876	Thomas Barr	Glasgow
26 July 1876	John Williams	Durham
1 Aug 1876	James Parris	Maidstone
14 Aug 1876	Richard Thompson	Liverpool
	William Fish	
21 Aug 1876	Steven McKeown	Armagh
25 Aug 1876	Christos Emanuel Baumbos	Cork
	Thomas Crowe	
29 Aug 1876	John Ebblethrift	Newgate
11 Dec 1876	Charles O'Donnell	Newgate
14 Dec 1876	Robert Browning	Cambridge
19 Dec 1876	Silas Barlow	Horsemonger
20 Dec 1876	John Green	Leicester
21 Dec 1876	William Flanagan	Manchester

2 Jan 1877	Isaac Marks	Horsemonger
12 Mar 1877	Henry Tidbury	Reading
	Francis Tidbury	
26 Mar 1877	William Clark	Lincoln
27 Mar 1877	John McKenna	Manchester
2 April 1877	James Bannister	Chester
17 April 1877	Frederick Edwin Baker	Warwick
31 July 1877	John Henry Starkey	Leicester
13 Aug 1877	Henry Leigh	Chester
14 Aug 1877	Caleb Smith	Horsemonger
21 Aug 1877	John Golding	Liverpool
	Patrick McGovern	
15 Oct 1877	John Lynch	Newgate
12 Nov 1877	Thomas Benjamin Pratt	Newgate
19 Nov 1877	William Hassell	Exeter
20 Nov 1877	Henry Marsh	Norwich
21 Nov 1877	Thomas Grey	Nottingham
23 Nov 1877	Cadwallader Jones	Dolgelly
27 Nov 1877	James Satchell	Leicester
	John William Swift	
	John Upton	
4 Feb 1878	George Piggott	Manchester
11 Feb 1878	James Caffyn	Winchester
12 Feb 1878	James Trickett	Liverpool
13 Feb 1878	John Brooks	Nottingham
1 April 1878	Henry Rowles	Oxford
15 April 1878	Vincent Knowles Walker	York
31 May 1878	Eugene Marie Chantrelle	Edinburgh
29 July 1878	Charles Joseph Revell	Chelmsford
30 July 1878	Robert Vest	Durham
12 Aug 1878	Thomas Cholerton	Nottingham
15 Aug 1878	Selina Wadge	Bodmin
3 Oct 1878	William McDonald	Cupar
8 Oct 1878	Thomas Smithers	Wandsworth
12 Nov 1878	John Patrick Byrne	Northampton
18 Nov 1878	Joseph Garcia	Usk
19 Nov 1878	James McGowan	Manchester
25 Nov 1878	Henry Gilbert	Huntingdon

10 Jan 1879	Thomas Cunceen	Limerick
4 Feb 1879	Stephen Gambrill	Maidstone
10 Feb 1879	Enoch Whiston	Worcester
11 Feb 1879	William McGuiness	Lancaster
25 Feb 1879	Charles Frederick Peace	Leeds
24 Mar 1879	James Simms	Newgate
12 May 1879	Edwin Smart	Gloucester
20 May 1879	William Cooper	Manchester
26 May 1879	Catherine Churchill	Taunton
27 May 1879	John Darcy	York
28 May 1879	Thomas Johnson	Liverpool
29 July 1879	Catherine Webster	Wandsworth
11 Aug 1879	Annie Tooke	Exeter
25 Aug 1879	James Dilley	Newgate
26 Aug 1879	John Ralph	Warwick
3 Dec 1879	Henry Bedingfield	Ipswich
5 Jan 1880	Charles Surety	Newgate
16 Jan 1880	Martin McHugo	Galway
17 Feb 1880	William Cassidy	Manchester
2 Mar 1880	Hugh Burns	Liverpool
	Patrick Kearnes	
22 Mar 1880	John Wingfield	Newgate
14 April 1880	Peter Conway	Omagh
10 May 1880	William Dumbleton	Aylesbury
11 May 1880	John Henry Wood	York
27 July 1880	Thomas Berry	Maidstone
16 Aug 1880	John Wakefield	Derby
16 Nov 1880	William Brownlees	Durham
20 Nov 1880	Thomas Wheeler	St.Albans
27 Nov 1880	William Joseph Diston	Bristol
13 Dec 1880	William Herbert	Newgate
	George Pavey	
21 Feb 1881	William Stanway	Chester
28 Feb 1881	Albert Robinson	Derby
17 May 1881	Albert Moore	Maidstone
23 May 1881	James Hall	Leeds
31 May 1881	Joseph Patrick McEntire	Liverpool
15 Aug 1881	Thomas Brown	Nottingham

23 Aug 1881	George Durling	Maidstone
21 Nov 1881	Alfred Gough	Derby
28 Nov 1881	John Aspinall Simpson	Manchester
29 Nov 1881	Percy Lefroy Mapleton	Lewes
30 Jan 1882	Charles Gerrish	Devizes
13 Feb 1882	Richard Templeton	Manchester
28 April 1882	George Henry Lamson	Wandsworth
16 May 1882	Thomas Fury	Durham
22 May 1882	William George Abigale	Norwich
23 May 1882	Osmond Otto Brand	Leeds
21 Aug 1882	William Turner	Liverpool
11 Sep 1882	Francis Hynes	Limerick
22 Sep 1882	Patrick Walsh	Galway
13 Nov 1882	William Meager Bartlett	Bodmin
28 Nov 1882	Edward Wheatfill	York
4 Dec 1882	Bernard Mullarkey	Liverpool
12 Dec 1882	Charles Taylor	Wandsworth
15 Dec 1882	Patrick Casey	Galway
	Miles Joyce	
	Patrick Joyce	
2 Jan 1883	Louisa Jane Taylor	Maidstone
15 Jan 1883	Patrick Higgins	Galway
17 Jan 1883	Michael Flynn	Galway
	Thomas Higgins	
23 Jan 1883	Thomas Barrett	Tralee
	Silvester Poff	
12 Feb 1883	Abraham Thomas	Manchester
19 Feb 1883	James Anderson	Lincoln
30 April 1883	Timothy O'Keefe	Cork
7 May 1883	Thomas Garry	Lincoln
8 May 1883	Patrick Carey	Chester
14 May 1883	Joseph Brady	Dublin
18 May 1883	Daniel Curley	Dublin
21 May 1883	Joseph Wedlake Taunton	
	George White	
23 May 1883	Henry Mullen	Glasgow
	Martin Scott	
28 May 1883	Michael Fagan	Dublin

2 Jun 1883	Thomas Caffrey	Dublin
9 Jun 1883	Timothy Kelly	Dublin
6 Aug 1883	James Burton	Durham

Appendix 3

The locations of executions carried out by William Marwood are listed below:

Marwood took part in one hundred and eighty executions. He had two executions as an assistant with William Calcraft, Michael Kennedy at Manchester on date December 30th, 1872 and James Connor at Kirkdale Prison, Liverpool, on September 8th, 1873.

Marwood worked with Incher on the occasions that needed two executioners i.e. doubles, until 1881 and then used Bartholomew Binns as an assistant until 1883 when Binns took over as Number One.

During Marwood's reign as Number One, there were fourteen double executions, three triples and one quadruple execution.

Place	Number of Executions
Armagh	1
Aylesbury	1
Belfast	1
Bodmin	2
Bristol	3
Cambridge	1
Cardiff	1
Chelmsford	2
Chester	4
Clonmel	1
Cork	3
Cupar	1
Derby	4
Devises	1
Dolgelly	1
Dublin	5
Dumbarton	1
Durham	12
Edinburgh	1
Exeter	3
Galway	8
Glasgow	4
Gloucester	1
Huntingdon	1
Ipswich	1
Jersey	1
Lancaster	3
Leeds	3
Leicester	5
Lewes	1